MW01610135

FAILPROOF CHILDREN

FAILPROOF CHILDREN

Dr. Ivan W. Fitzwater

MANDEL PUBLICATIONS
a division of the
Management Development Institute
San Antonio, Texas

Library of Congress Cataloging in Publication Data

Fitzwater, Ivan W.
  Failproof Children.

1. Parenting	2. Parent and child	3. Child psychology
4. Success	5. Failure (Psychology)	I. Title

HQ755.8.F58	1979	649′.1	82-192705

ISBN 0-941420-02-7

Printed in the United States of America

Original production, including design and illustrations, by Summit Publishing Co., Inc., San Antonio. Illustrated by David Forks.

Second printing, 1985, by Hart Graphics, Inc., Austin, Texas

To my wife, Kathleen,
and to our children,
Sidney, Elizabeth and Martha,
for making life
an exciting
and satisfying adventure

TABLE OF CONTENTS

FOREWORD

FOREWORD

It is characteristic in every era of human history to find adults severely critical of the next generation. A scathing denunciation of young people done in the time of Socrates varies little from the articles written about children in today's newspapers. I often wonder about this righteous indignation on the part of adults. After all, we are condemning our own handiwork. Whatever our children may be, it is we who have borne them, molded them and, in the last analysis, are totally responsible for the results.

What would happen if the older generation confronted this reality? Suppose we admitted that all of the problems of today's youth were **adult-caused?** More important, suppose we decided to change *our* behavior in the future so we could stop being the culprits? Wouldn't this positive approach bring a positive result just as negative now begets negative?

This train of thought gave rise to the failproof theory, which actually emphasizes achievement and ignores failure. It is accomplished by always assigning tasks which can be done successfully—never ones which cause failure. A pattern of success then emerges which grows into a strong self-image and a habit of succeeding.

The theory is new only in title and scope of proposed application. Teachers have long known that highly motivated students succeed if the work assigned is appropriate in terms of the degree of difficulty. But in our world of standardized expectations, mass teaching and stereotyped comparisons, the individualized assignment of tasks is rarely done.

One exception to this is in physical therapy where small progressive steps of exercise are used to bring the injured muscles back to health. Minute achievements are built, one upon the other, as rapidly as possible until a goal is accomplished, but the steps are never greater than the ability of the learner to complete them successfully.

This therapy for disabled people is a pattern which will work for *all* people, including children. Therefore, I propose a system of teaching built upon this concept to ensure success in all children without regard to innate ability.

All writers tend to disclaim their theories by saying "this will not work in all cases—reader discretion is necessary." Let me be the exception. I pledge to you it *will* work in all cases—if you are willing to do your part as parents or teachers. I believe in you; I ask you to believe in me.

Ivan W. Fitzwater

San Antonio
January, 1979

Chapter 1

THE FAILPROOF THEORY

Instances of child failure are, in reality, due to adult failure—the *blame* is just placed incorrectly by observers who do not have, or do not *want* to have, the facts. It is the defenseless children who become victims of parents and other adults who, through ignorance rather than intent, are the ones who prevent the success of a youngster. For example, we call the child born out of wedlock *illegitimate,* thus placing blame for the situation on a helpless infant when, actually, two adults violated society's code of behavior. Though extreme, this illustration describes a concept which transfers perfectly to child failure.

Children fail when the tasks they are asked to perform are too difficult based upon previous training and experience, or if they have not been stimulated to want to do the task. If care is given to selection of tasks so that success is always possible, and if attention is given to creating a climate of desire to succeed, then failure can be prevented in any child. Obviously, a climate of complete motivation and the attention to task selection has to be done consistently, and it has to be perfect at every step for complete failure prevention. This utopia has rarely been achieved in the past, but the concept is valid and worthy of study because when success and failure are viewed in this way, a whole new approach is taken to child rearing. The extent to which adults succeed in implementing the concept will determine the degree of failproofing the child receives. This places the challenge on *adults* rather than children—a dramatic change of emphasis but a proper one.

Success and Failure Are Relative Terms

For a man who loves to play tennis, the thrill of competition and a chance to be outdoors are things which make him happy. By Wimbledon players' standards, he would be a failure; by the standards of a beginning player, he is a great success. He is the same person in both cases, but his success as a player is relative, depending upon the standard of measure being used.

The same is true of a child doing arithmetic in school. A boy or girl could be a great success working second-grade arithmetic but a failure at fifth-grade arithmetic. Adjusting the level of work makes the difference, assuming that the children want to do arithmetic in the first place. Determination of success or failure rests with selection of the tasks based upon ability and maturity of the learners. In the past, failure was viewed as students being one hundred per cent wrong; the failproofing theory implies that *tasks* are one hundred per cent wrong if motivated students cannot perform them.

Also in a consideration of the relativity of success and failure, there must be a consideration of goals. In the tennis example, even when the man lost a game, his goals were reached if he played for exercise and fun. These can be accomplished without making a winning score. In fact, he could lose every time in terms of score but succeed every time in terms of goals.

The point of this is to describe another example of the relationship between success and failure. Desire, task difficulty and definition of goals play a greater role in success or failure than the choice of game or player. As parents and teachers, we can failproof children by controlling these elements to ensure success.

Selection of Tasks Is Crucial

Here is an equation which describes the failproofing concept:

MOTIVATED CHILD + APPROPRIATE TASK = SUCCESS

It is obvious from this equation that task selection is crucial (so is motivation, but this will be dealt with in a later chapter). The key to task selection is progression in exactly the right amount to prevent boredom but never too much to be beyond the ability of the child to perform correctly. This is easiest to describe using physical tasks as examples, but the concept is valid in the affective (behaviorial) domain as well. Let us say, for instance, that a child is able to perform a successful high jump over a bar set four feet one inch high. We set as a goal four feet one and a half inches, to be cleared at the end of a week's practice. This is growth, but we know that it is a possible goal also, based upon thorough study of the situation. The motivated child achieves the goal in the time allotted and is declared a success.

Suppose this same child had been given a four-foot, three-inch hurdle just because he or she happened to be a particular age or in a particular grade? The task would have been beyond the child's ability and experience at this point in time—the result being failure.

When tasks are always selected properly, failure is avoided. Enough progression is employed to cause forward movement, but goals are adjusted constantly to prevent failure. The assumption is consistently embraced that growth and success depend upon task selection and not artificial standards such as average achievement of children based upon age or any other criterion.

What Growth Will This Produce?

Perhaps a good way to answer this question would be to turn it around and say: What happens when work is beyond one's ability and failure results? It is obvious—continual frustration over an extended period of time causes discouragement and lack of self-confidence. This lack of confidence becomes a self-fulfilling prophecy: lack of confidence lowers likelihood of success; less success causes less confidence, etc., etc. The image of self deteriorates, failure becomes easier, and success rare or impossible. The failproof system keeps success assured, confidence growing, and evokes a positive self-fulfilling prophecy. Success becomes a constant and failure the rarity. Positive self-image is strengthened and reinforced and the spiral continues upward.

What growth will this produce? It boggles the mind to think what might happen if success were constant and failure eliminated. Various professionals to whom the idea has been proposed shake their heads at first saying, "Impossible to achieve!" But once they think of the concept hypothetically, they agree that growth might be dramatically accelerated beyond anything heretofore imagined. Smart students could leap ahead in this success atmosphere; less bright students could progress relative to their ability but faster than ever before. All could benefit markedly when subjected to failproof teaching.

Image Is Most Important

Depending upon his or her self-image, the same person will perform differently. Failproofing rules out all standards other than progression based upon one's own ability and experience. This ensures a constant, positive self-image and maximum growth. The following stories illustrate the point:

The first-grade teachers in a large elementary school grouped their students according to their readiness for reading. One teacher had a group of very immature students who were not nearly ready to read because they lacked the mental and physical development. In an ordinary class, these students might have been called slow in comparison to more mature learners. Fortunately, this school and this particular teacher understood that time would take care of the maturity, that these kids would become good readers unless a poor self-image were to develop causing them to believe they were not good readers. The teacher knew that attitudes about oneself become imprinted upon the mind, so she made sure her children's self-images were protected by choosing failproof tasks as "reading" activities for them. Coloring and listening to exciting stories constituted their "reading," and the teacher used praise and

3

reassurance to constantly let them know they were doing well. In a few months, these children read as well as the other pupils because their teacher knew that maturity tends to cause achievement to plateau. Failure in those early months was averted by proper selection of tasks and self-images remained positive. The image which had been cultivated—the positive self-image—became the self-fulfilling prophecy, and the students became readers as soon as their physical maturity reached the appropriate level.

Another example of image protection and its importance is illustrated in this example:

A mother kept precious and fragile heirlooms out of reach of her young children. Occasionally, she would take them down from their high shelf and, holding them securely, would let her young child touch, or "play," with them. Because of the care taken, there were no traumatic situations resulting from valuable objects being broken.

A less-wise mother, insensitive to the importance of early self-images and the failproofing concept, left precious keepsakes exposed. The normal, vigorous activity of children resulted in broken objects, harsh criticism, and severe feelings of guilt for these youngsters. In this family, a perfectly normal child developed a self-concept of clumsiness. An ordinary accident evoked a statement like: "That's just the way I am; I've always been clumsy." The prophecy was continually reinforced and became a lifetime image and expectation. The children in the examples differ very little; parental behavior was the variable which caused self-images of success or failure.

Failproofing: Is It Possible?

It can and has been demonstrated in microcosm that the concept of failproofing is valid. When the idea is considered as a teaching approach for all children, the prediction is often made that it will fail because of human nature—that no parents or teachers are going to be conscientious and dedicated enough to follow through to the point necessary for total success. Another summary might be more accurate: It will work to the extent that it is faithfully tried and perfected. This is true of most endeavors in the human arena. A weight-reducing diet brings weight loss every time it is properly followed without deviation. Would the fact that many persons fail to succeed in weight loss because of their own weakness be a reason to condemn weight-reducing diets?

A more productive approach to failproofing is to try the concept, recognizing that perfection will not be achieved immediately or perhaps ever. Gains will be commensurate with dedication and perseverance in implementing the idea and THIS is growth. The theory works in direct proportion to the success of the parents and teachers in their implementation of their roles.

SUMMARY CHECK LIST
Three Examples of the Theory in Practice
Example One

A father wants his four-year-old son to learn to catch a ball. They talk about the fun of playing ball and do other things to build motivation in the child. The boy becomes enthusiastic about learning to play, so they buy a ball—a large one because this is easier for a young child to handle at this stage of his development.

At first, the boy is merely handed the ball rather than catching a thrown one. Each time the ball is held in his hands, or even between hands and chest, there is praise by the father. As skill develops, the father backs farther and farther away so that catching becomes more real. A dropped ball never brings criticism; patience and constant encouragement are the rules. Growth comes progressively in an atmosphere of fun and success.

Example Two

A young girl has a problem of getting along with other children. Fighting is a constant occurrence. The parents decide to take steps to correct the situation, but rather than criticize, they decide to use progressive growth steps to correct the situation.

They suggest that she will have more fun by being friendlier with her playmates. They point out how much better she will feel by playing without fighting, and they set up a program to achieve this: Every day she gets through without a fight she is rewarded in some way which is pleasing to her. Setbacks are quickly overcome by setting new goals. As the periods without fights grow longer, goals are raised and rewards increased until being cooperative becomes the predominant behavior.

Example Three

A teenager wants to win a part in a school play, but the selected character part requires memorizing hundreds of pages. The task is so awesome that the youngster is intimidated to the point of not even wanting to audition. A wise coach overcomes the feeling of intimidation by requiring only a few pages be memorized for tryouts. Our teenager wins the part and, after being chosen, masters a few additional pages each week. The praise given as each portion is completed provides impetus to complete the next, slightly larger, segment without frustration. Soon, the whole part is memorized and satisfaction and success result.

Chapter 2

TURNING KIDS ON

Failproofing rests upon the dual premise of proper task selection and motivation. The secret to its success is to select a progression of tasks so that a new experience is always within the child's capability but, at the same time, an improvement over past performance. To keep from having one unsuccessful attempt result in failure, boundaries are used to define success. Example: The goal is to learn the multiplication table of three by the end of a given week. Mistakes made while reaching the ultimate goal are discounted as long as the overall objective is completed by the stated time. Since the goal has been chosen with complete assurance that it can be achieved without failure, success will occur if motivation is present in the learner.

As task assigners, not only must parents and teachers be astute in proper task selection, but they must possess a thorough knowledge of how motivation occurs in learners. Indeed, the difference between success and failure literally rests upon how well the motivational phase is accomplished. Teachers who say: "My students don't want to learn" are overlooking a basic fact. Students are not supposed to want to learn instinctively or spontaneously. The first job of any parent or teacher is to motivate the learner. "Turning kids on" is the first step in mastering any new subject and is the first obligation of any parent or teacher who truly wants to help kids grow.

Very successful teachers (or parents) are the ones who create in learners strong enthusiasm and desire for learning. This true story illustrates the point: A young man went off to college to study law. His enthusiasm was unbridled, and he saw no reason to study anything not directly connected with that discipline. Much to his chagrin, he was immediately faced with the requirement of a four-credit course in geology. His attitude was one of disgust; he approached the course with anything but a positive attitude. Resentful of the requirement, he was about as negative as any learner could be.

A month later, the change was remarkable. The pre-law student seemed interested in nothing except geology! (In fact, rocks are an abiding interest of his even to this day.) His professor, accustomed to reluctant students, was proficient in the art of motivation, and he did what was necessary to stimulate his students. He knew the first rule of any good teacher—get the kids intensely interested and teaching will be much more productive.

What Causes Motivation on the Part of Learners?

There is no simple answer to the question of what it is that generates effective motivation, but the adult who wishes to be successful as a motivator should bear in mind certain facts:

1. *Enthusiasm is infectious.*

In the area of learning known as the affective domain (as opposed to cognitive or fact-learning), most attitudes are absorbed from others, particularly adults. The teacher or parent who is enthusiastic about any given idea or topic will find children adopting that attitude. This is why teachers who dearly love their subject have students who catch this same feeling of intense interest. This is why children, particularly at an early age, reflect the interests of parents. The lawyer who loves his work and talks about it in an exciting way before his children is likely to have youngsters who want to study law. Conversely, parents who talk about how terrible their work is tend to unconsciously guide their children into other pursuits unless the children are economically trapped.

Farm children are a good example. If parents obviously love farming, if they share that love while involving their children in that vocation, then the children will want to make a career in agriculture. If, instead, the parents evidence negative feelings, share only the drudgery and their discontent, children yearn to escape the farm. As parents and teachers, we motivate positively and negatively more by our own attitudes than anything else.

2. *Success breeds success; failure breeds failure.*

A lesson which must be learned by adults is that human beings, especially young ones, grow a little each time they experience success and regress a little each time failure is experienced. This is really the whole idea behind failproofing and a good summary for the entire concept. Rather than repeat in short form the points made throughout the book, it will suffice to say that constant success and feelings of accomplishment will be our goals for children.

3. *Rewards are essential.*

The learner will make greatest progress when such achievement is rewarded. The reward does not have to be large or of great intrinsic value. It does not even have to be a tangible thing, but some form of recognition is crucial. Caution should be exercised, however.

Overrewarding where the value of the award exceeds reason can be a negative force. The act of recognition on the part of an adult or adults is the important element.

4. *Momentum is helpful.*

Just as objects tend to continue in the same direction when in motion, so do human beings. Kids moving in a positive direction tend to continue positive growth; kids headed in the "wrong" direction tend to continue that way. Young people who feel the momentum of growth and progress (as reflected by attitudes of adults) will make the greatest progress.

5. *Praise stimulates growth.*

Every time an action is praised, the urge is to repeat it and do it better. Praise does not have to be effusive but consistency is important. A pat on the back, a smile, a comment like "well done!" will accelerate progress.

6. *Maximum growth occurs in an atmosphere of security.*

Human beings are more apt to try new things when they know that defeat will not have a long-term, negative effect. Children must feel so secure about their parents' love that they are willing to undertake risks and adventures—both actions which are necessary for mastering new challenges. Home should be a warm, comfortable haven which is always there to return to after the child's adventuring.

7. *The existence of a family-team motivates.*

When people feel they are an integral part of a larger unit, it gives them a sense of identity and recognition, stimulating growth. Since the whole is greater than the sum of its parts, the solidarity of the family which operates as a team will provide greater stimulation. The team feeling which is experienced in sports can also exist in the family. The vigor so acquired is very helpful as a positive force in growth. The natural feeling on the part of a youngster that the other family members will stand behind him—that his "Daddy can beat up anybody"—illustrates family-team feeling so important for the young child. Let us hope that a positive self-image will be firmly ingrained before the youngster learns his dad's real fighting ability!

Parental Modesty
Is Required for Child Motivation

A frequent deterrent to motivation of children is the overpowering personalities of their parents. Children who feel intimidated by the achievements or dominant characteristics of their parents can withdraw rather than push ahead. Feeling inadequate due to the successes of their parents, they may tend to lead passive rather than active lives. Parents must be, on the one hand, good examples to be imitated, but they must also be willing to practice modesty and self-effacement so that children can shine through the age barrier. Their ability to share the spotlight is essential.

Sibling Rivalry Can Be Important

Just as relations with parents can be positive or negative in terms of motivation, so can relations between brother and sister. A general rule would be to have as little comparison of children as possible and as much individualization as possible.

In addition to elimination of comparison, it is well for each child to have a special area of accomplishment which is his or hers alone. If one child excels as a dancer while another excels as a musician, this creates for each a comfortable area of accomplishment which makes possible individual identity, so essential for positive self-image and motivation.

If both children pursue the same activity, age differences immediately cause difficulty. Either the younger child is frustrated because he or she lacks as much development, or he *is* able to compete equally in spite of the age difference, which causes resentment on the part of the older one. There is potential negative reinforcement for one of the two, in either case.

Fear Must Be Prevented or Corrected

For motivation to occur, such things as negative self-stereotyping and fearfulness must be minimized or eliminated. The self-stereotyping is easiest to demonstrate because people with similar abilities achieve differently, based upon their self-images. It is a veritable truth: Persons who say "I can't" usually mean "I won't." The difference is simply a person's stereotyping of himself—the same manner of stereotyping that occurs in his views of others.

A more difficult phenomenon to overcome is fear. If children or adults consciously or unconsciously sense danger to personal or psychological self, they are reluctant to go forward to try new things that are necessary for growth and success.

This has much to say to parents and other adults who work with young people:

1. Children must be protected from trauma which can cause future fear.

2. Fear is not proper punishment in correcting behavior or preventing future misbehavior.

3. Fear which does develop must be eliminated through counseling or other appropriate steps.

4. Fears held by adults are readily absorbed by children.

We are only briefly touching upon an area which could be the basis for an entire book, but here is an example to illustrate one result of fear as it relates to motivation:

Children learn fear just as they learn other attitudes, of course. One five-year-old had learned fear of water because of a traumatic incident three years earlier when she had fallen into a wading pool and choked on water drawn into her nose and mouth. This terrifying experience, coupled with the late beginning of swimming instruction (five years of age is considered late), made an introduction to the water very difficult. Her fear killed all natural interest in swimming; what's more, the child fought against swimming instruction when the parents offered the idea.

Motivating the child to learn this vital skill required, as a prerequisite, the elimination of the fear. Gradual induction by an understanding instructor eventually provided the fear reduction and security which permitted development of the desire to learn to swim. Failure on the part of the parents to understand fear and its relationship to motivation could have led to lack of achievement or, worse yet, could have added to the trauma.

SUMMARY CHECK LIST

1. A home where enthusiasm is prevalent is essential.
2. Success gives the best foundation for future sucess.
3. Praise must be given every time it is justified.
4. Psychological security comes through unselfish love.
5. Maintain momentum if behavior is in the right direction, change momentum if it is in the wrong direction.
6. Operate the family on a team basis.
7. Don't overpower children with parental accomplishments.
8. Be sensitive to making sibling rivalry a positive motivational force.
9. Eliminate feelings of fear.
10. Reward achievement rather than punish failure.

Chapter 3

ASSERTIVENESS WINS

A young girl is planning to try out for cheerleader at her high school. There is always keen competition for these positions, and the final stage in the competition is an election by the student body involving those girls who have reached the finals by virtue of their cheerleading skills. One day, the girl hears that a competitor is spreading rumors about her that might hurt her chances of becoming one of those elected. Very distressed and feeling she must do something immediately, she considers three possible plans of action.

The first is just to wait and hope that the other girl will stop spreading the rumors and that the damage already done will not be severe. In this way, she can pretend that she has not heard of the rumors or that she does not care. She realizes that there are risks involved because the rumors may continue or even be enlarged, and her chances of winning the cheerleader election may be affected. There is also the danger that her lack of response may give credence to the rumors.

She considers a second plan of action involving a direct confrontation. She can arrange to be in the school cafeteria when the other girl is there with a number of their mutual friends. At that moment, she will tell her that she knows about the rumors and that they are untrue and must stop immediately. She will also try to make her attack strong enough to get her to admit her wrongdoing or at least convince the other students that the other girl has been the offender. This plan also involves risks because the crowd may sympathize with the other girl, or the strength of the attack might cause the other students to be even more convinced of the truth of the rumors. There is even a chance that the other girl has not been really spreading rumors at all—that she is innocent.

A third approach is considered and ultimately chosen as the one to be employed. First, she will neither ignore the problem nor will she attack belligerently. Instead, she chooses a middle-of-the-road approach. She will confront the girl privately and express her intense concern. She will not accuse her but she will tell her what she has heard and request an explanation. Standing firm and insisting upon fair treatment, she will not take stronger action than is necessary, but she will not allow herself to be mistreated. Selecting this approach is the most effective—it gets the job done with a minimum of risk in terms of possible side effects.

Passive, Aggressive and Assertive Behavior

The student in this illustration considered three possible behaviors in an attempt to solve her problem. The first, which involved waiting and withdrawing, would be an example of passive behavior. The second, which was a frontal attack, would be considered aggressive. The third type of behavior, however, involved direct action to solve the problem, but it was done in an atmosphere of calm, contemplative firmness. Only the amount of power necessary to solve the problem was employed. Overkill was avoided, as was capitulation. This is the attitude with the greatest possibility for lifetime success.

Wholesome Assertiveness Is the Key

The skill which we must teach young people might be termed *wholesome assertiveness*. This describes a mind-set, causing a person to choose a firmness of personality in which to prevent others from abusing or taking advantage of him. At the same time, he must not become rude or offensive to the point of being obnoxious. The fine line between assertiveness and aggressiveness is the most difficult to define. Children understand passiveness as opposed to aggressiveness more easily than between the two levels of active behavior.

A key to understanding the concept of wholesome assertiveness would be to "insist upon fair treatment from everyone, but use no more force than is necessary to ensure your rights." For example, children should be taught to expect merchandise equal to the money they spend. When something is faulty when purchased (not due to negligence or mistreatment on the part of the buyer), the child should be taught to return the item and insist upon a full refund. At the same time, he/she must be taught to be pleasant, not raise his voice or indulge in emotional outbursts. Gentle, quiet firmness, continued until justice is done, is the most productive approach.

The failproof concept of appropriate task selection and gradual growth is extremely important here. A child cannot be sheltered and permitted to be passive for a period of years and then, all of a sudden, be expected to be assertive. Exposure to the world is essential in the very early years. Techniques must have continual adult guidance, but children can insist upon taking turns at play, and they can pay for their own purchases as soon as they can count money. These are but two examples of steps which help to develop wholesome assertiveness.

Selection of Playmates Is Important

An area of a child's life which profoundly affects mental attitude is the peer environment. Young people readily take psychological cues from their contemporaries and inadvertently begin to play roles which can become behavior patterns. For example, if a child plays with other children who are older, there is a tendency to adopt submissive responses. If the group average is much younger than he, the tendency is to dominate and assume leadership without earning the position. Both attitudes are potentially damaging. The general guideline is to have children play with others close to their own age.

Consider, for instance, the effect of widely differing ages in athletic competition. Assuming he has no unusual sports skill, the child who is much younger will neither be a winner in individual sports nor a leader in team sports. The role which is played because of less physical development leads to negative attitude development. Since attitude is far more important than anything else, the result of the uneven physical competition is harmful to the positive mental attitude which is crucial to success.

Teacher Cooperation Is Necessary

Most basic attitudes are established by the time children enter school, but some consideration of teacher actions is still warranted. In their efforts to maintain group control, teachers are in a position of dangerously "culturing out" the wholesome assertiveness which is a natural gift. The teacher who mistakes activity for misbehavior and quiet for learning will thwart growth in assertiveness. It is necessary to teach children to stand in line, hold up their hands to speak and be quiet at certain times, but learning only occurs *when the learner* is *physically or mentally active.* Oppression of activity too much of the time teaches passiveness.

School is a socialization process, and students should be learning how to live with other people. This mandates the teaching of social skills such as cooperation and group needs in relation to individual desires. For example, teachers must be very careful to distinguish between tact and passiveness because the two are easily confused. Children must be taught both concepts simultaneously and clearly because both are essential skills for living.

SUMMARY CHECK LIST

1. Help the child distinguish between passive, aggressive and assertive behavior.

2. Teach wholesome assertiveness—no more force than necessary to receive fair treatment.

3. Let small children make purchases and handle transactions to gain familiarity with such activity.

4. Select playmates carefully on other than geographical grounds. Wide differences in age can cause passiveness.

5. Provide socialization experiences which distinguish clearly between tact and timidity.

Chapter 4

A SUCCESS ORIENTATION

The Enemy Inside

There's an enemy out to get you —
    He'll destroy you if he can.
His name is Lack of Confidence
    And he's lurking in every man.

Whenever you face a challenge,
    He will whisper in your ear
And tell you all the risks involved,
    And the things that you should fear.

But there's one sure way to defeat him:
    It's to constantly say, "I can,"
To know in your heart from the very start
    You're equal to any man.

Then you venture when others are timid,
    See hope when others despair.
You rely on yourself; you don't give up.
    You fight hard and long and fair.

You don't spend your time complaining
    About luck (how it passed you by).
And you don't make any excuses
    For the times that you just didn't try.

This positive way of thinking
    Gives a key that will set you free:
While the mass of men stand idly by,
    Your dreams are realities.

Life is a self-fulfilling prophecy. Never was this better illustrated than in the case of one man who appeared as a major speaker at a large national sales convention. Severely physically handicapped by a crippling disease which struck him in the prime of his life, his body was twisted and gnarled by the effects of the disease, and he was confined to a wheelchair every waking hour. But his attitude was so positive that the handicap did little except bring out the best in him. He believed he could succeed, and this belief was fulfilled completely.

The audience was enrapt as he related his story: "I was twenty-three years old and an insurance salesman when this disease struck me. I had been doing about average as a salesman so, at first, I decided to give up. Certainly, I thought, it would be impossible to continue with any degree of success. But that was a bad decision—being crippled is bad enough, but being crippled and bored is even worse.

"I decided to see what I *could* accomplish, even with this limited physical condition. Today I am the top salesman in my firm, and it is not because anyone gives me breaks; I accomplished this on my own. I always wanted to write a book but didn't ever seem to have time. When you realize that time might be very limited, you stop procrastinating— you don't put things off till later. My book is now published; so is a second, and I'm working at the rate of one new one per year. I always wanted to make speeches but I was too shy. My new success as a salesman and author has given me the confidence to speak, and now I make a hundred speeches a year and $50,000 for doing them.

"I used to begin each day by worrying about what I had done wrong in the past and what might go wrong in the future. Consequently, I never lived in the present. I don't do that anymore. Now I start each day by thanking God for another day and praying that I can accomplish all of the exciting plans I've made."

This man illustrates what can happen when an individual plans to succeed and lives accordingly. Success orientation can accelerate the accomplishments of anyone; the technique is not mysterious, nor does it require a great deal beyond commitment which comes from positive attitude. Success orientation exemplifies the failproof approach at its best because one accomplishment is built upon another in rapid progression.

Positive Attitude Is the Key

People vary little in physical or mental ability but dramatically in their accomplishments. If brains and brawn don't necessarily make the difference, what does? Obviously, the important ingredient is attitude. Parents can do no more important a service than to help children develop the most positive attitude possible. This means a positive self-image; it means liking oneself.

Children learn what they live. An environment of optimism, enthusiasm and happiness resulting from accomplishment brings the best results, so parents must place these goals in high priority so that children can live in the best psychological environment possible.

Plan for Success by Setting Goals

Setting goals and making plans for reaching them are essential to success. As soon as a goal is accomplished, another must be set because man is by nature a goal-seeking animal and is unhappy unless working toward some accomplishment. Parents must teach children the habit of planning and the specific goals to be accomplished before a task is begun.

These simple planning techniques will carry over into larger things:

"Let's stop and think ahead how we are going to proceed before we start to build this birdhouse," says Father, acknowledging the need for plans.

Then the simple plan is written down, including a picture of the finished birdhouse. Tools and materials needed are written down, too. The lessons learned from such simple tasks will carry over into the larger challenges of life.

Life Must Be Kept in Perspective

A child who grows up in a home where everything is provided runs the risk of taking things for granted. This can lead to a lack of appreciation for life's blessings so that unhappiness comes in the midst of plenty. For example, good health can be taken for granted if illness is never experienced or if the child never knows someone who is a victim of illness.

Morbid reminders of the illness in the world would not be helpful; at the same time, perspective can be lost if no mention is made of the things for which we should be grateful. Rather than parental preaching though, a better method would be to use the opportunity to help those in the world who are less fortunate. Not only is it the humanitarian thing to do, but it is also constructive for young people to become increasingly aware of those who need help and then to spend some time helping them. The young person who contributes time on weekends in volunteer service to poor or sick people has little trouble keeping life in perspective. This appreciation for life's blessings gives a positive thrust to the one who serves and, as such, becomes "bread cast upon the waters."

Defeat Must Be Overcome Routinely

Any person who attempts to do many things will experience defeat. Like the proverbial turtle who "makes progress only when he sticks his neck out," success requires exposure to possible defeat. The proper focus is to realize that defeat at any single point is but a minute particle when considered in the context of a lifetime.

Defeat is necessary to keep people alert in doing their best. It in no way lessens the value of the person concerned and it doesn't make him a loser. Quite the contrary is true: our most successful people, such as the great inventors, failed far more times than they succeeded.

Young people need to understand that the statistics on success are always in their favor if they will persevere. It has been estimated that ninety-five per cent of all people never try a given task a second time if it is a voluntary situation that has failed the first time. A person who is willing to try a second time, however, has eliminated ninety-five per cent of the potential competition; a third time, ninety-eight per cent of the competition! "Getting up one more time than you are knocked down," as one speaker has defined success, will overcome defeat and virtually assure eventual success.

Children must be taught this attitude, and they must see it demonstrated in life. They must feel confident enough to try and secure enough to fail. Perseverance is not an instinct but a learned response which is developed through practice and experience.

Time Must Be Profitably Managed

Time is a unique resource which must be utilized to the maximum for success. It is the great leveler because everybody gets the same amount and everybody gets all there is. If any person accomplishes more than another, it is usually because the successful person has learned to manage time more effectively.

The best description of the uniqueness of time is in the classic example of the "Bank of Time" by an unknown author:

> If you had a bank that credited your account each morning with $86,400 that carried over no balance from day to day, allowed you to keep no cash in account, and every evening canceled whatever part of the amount you failed to use during the day, just what would you do? Draw out every cent, of course!
>
> Well, you have such a bank and its name is *Time*. Every morning it credits you with 86,400 seconds. Every night it rules off, as lost, whatever part of this sum you have failed to invest to good purposes. It allows no overdrafts. Each day it opens a new account for you; each night it burns the record of the day. If you fail to use the day's deposits, the loss is yours. There's no going back; there's no drawing against tomorrow. You must live in the present — on today's deposits. Invest it so as to get from it the utmost in health, happiness and success.

A proper attitude toward time is essential for success. This does not mean rushing or overworking as in the case of workaholism. It does mean planning to make the best use of time. Dedicated work periods, planned recreation and fun, and adequate rest form the cycle of success with respect to time. There is time for everything in life if time is not taken for granted.

At the beginning of each day, a simple plan should be written down for that day. For a school-age youngster, this would include school obligations, a period for relaxation, mealtime with the family and a definite time to begin homework. Some time just to loaf would be included after the work is done and before the established bedtime. Only a true crisis should interfere with bedtime—and then, only on rare occasions.

The Symbolic Family Motto

The unaccountable fact that life tends to respond to our expectations can work to the advantage of those who exploit this phenomenon, and one excellent means of doing so is in the adoption of an expression of ideals—a family motto. Not necessarily complicated or even sophisticated—just positive—such a symbol will unify the group in that each member will be supportive of the successes of every other member. The motto used by one family was printed in large letters, framed and hung on the wall for all to see. As the children grew, *Never say "I can't"; always say "I'll try!"* was often repeated when challenges arose. The children grew up and left home and the sign was retired to the father's study, but the motto was not forgotten. One of the children became a teacher, moved to a distant city, and was assigned to a school where children had great needs.

The teacher's father had an occasion to visit her school one day and was pleased to hear from the principal how the students were responding to this young, relatively inexperienced teacher. Stepping into her classroom, he saw why. Prominently displayed at the front of the room was a newly engraved plaque with those oft-repeated words:

Never say "I can't"; always say "I'll try!"

The torch of positive thinking was being passed.

SUMMARY CHECK LIST

1. Realize how much difference a positive attitude makes.

2. Plan for the future, but learn to live one day at a time.

3. Recognize the importance of goals for people of all ages.

4. Keep life in perspective; record and recite the blessings of life.

5. Teach the statistics relative to perseverance.

6. Recognize the uniqueness of time and learn to manage it profitably.

7. Establish, and use, a positive family motto.

Chapter 5

CRITICAL STAGES
IN PARENT-CHILD COMMUNICATION

The success-provoking message which must be communicated from parent to offspring varies little throughout life, but the techniques for transmission do change. The message which must be constantly sent and received is: "I love you, I accept you, I am proud of you just because you are YOU." This gives the child a foundation which never falters, a refuge to which he or she can retreat when temporary setbacks occur. It is a haven to which the inquisitive, experimenting young one can repair and take stock in order to venture again. The security blanket of unconditional acceptance is an absolute must in the failproofing of children.

The message is constant; yet methods of sending and receiving must be adjusted to fit maturity levels and current emotional feelings of sender and receiver. A tired infant does not respond to the same communication techniques as a postadolescent. Neither does a disappointed parent send messages in the same way as an elated parent. Many other obstacles can get in the way. Reassuring a child of parental acceptance just when the child has broken a rule requires sending a message which says: "I love *you* but not the misbehavior." If the child feels loss of love or acceptance, something far more important than an incident of misbehavior is at issue. A deep scar could result, with long-term negative implications, through poor communication of specific intent.

The Basic Communication Model

All communication, whether oral, written or non-verbal (body language), occurs through a basic model. There is a sender, some sort of medium through which the message goes, and a receiver. All elements are essential if communication is to occur; but, without a doubt, the most essential part is the receiver. In fact, whatever is *actually* received is what is communicated. No matter what the intent of the sender, the message received is all that really counts in the last analysis.

Why is this so, and why do messages become garbled in the communication process? Basically, it is because messages are sent in code. The senders do not consciously disguise their messages, but coding occurs because of human factors. The sender chooses words, inflection and gestures out of a background of experiences. The message is clear to the sender, but because each person is an individual human being, unique words and symbols are chosen which reflect *that* person's knowledge and feelings and not necessarily those of the receiver.

The message is thus encoded and sent forth through a medium of exchange (sight, sound, etc.) where there is the possibility of interference or distortion. Then the receiver is reached; but here, too, the message goes through an encoder which is programmed by the experiences, feelings, and current emotional state of that person. Whatever finally filters through this whole system is the message perceived—and this is the crucial part.

All persons, parents especially, need to understand this communication model. If emphasis is upon "message sent" rather than "message received," much poor communication will result. It is incumbent upon the sender to know what is actually being received. This means the receiver must be understood, feedback must be used and the choice of sending-medium considered. Parents must be very sensitive to the maturity level, emotional state and level of fatigue of the recipient when messages are being sent.

Incidentally, this same consideration would improve communication between parents, which would eventually also help children. There are periods during the day—and week—when complete communication will occur best and periods when it is most difficult. For example, early in the morning is not usually a good time for husbands and wives to discuss mutual shortcomings. Emotion can take over and enlarge the problems, thus generating far more heat than light.

Communicating with Infants

It might be assumed that communication with the newborn or the child-in-arms is unimportant, but it may well be the most crucial time. Many theories have been advanced about the ability of infants to perceive the world around them, but most agree that intense communication does occur. Some child specialists feel that nursing babies is more important from the standpoint of communication than nutrition. We know that the brain is an amazing, complicated storage system upon which lifetime behavior is based. A great amount of this stored information is in the subconscious realm. How much storing occurs during the early months of life can be debated, but each new experiment seems to point to even greater importance of these early contacts.

For instance, in studies conducted in hospital nurseries and in orphanages, it has been established that babies who received little or no nurturing were not as healthy, physically or mentally, as other infants who did. Those who were rocked, who were held more often than just for caring for vital needs by attendants, were happier and grew faster.

Based upon present knowledge, then, it should be assumed that basic feelings of acceptance or rejection by the world are developed just after birth. These can be modified later in life, but modification is always more difficult than original teaching. Feelings of acceptance and security are vital, so parents must plan to provide strong positive input. This means BOTH parents must hold the infant physically close. Body warmth, voices and touching become connectors which transmit the impression that this organism is wanted and desired as a part of the family unit. Touching will be an important communicating technique throughout life but never more important than with the infant.

The child of several years demonstrates the secure feeling of mother's arms by retreating to them readily when afraid or when injured. This is natural and healthy, and the child should not be rejected at these times. The mother (or father!) who admonishes him with "Stop acting like a baby!" or "You're too big to cry" is, in a sense, rejecting him. If he thought he were too big to cry, he wouldn't. So her reaction to his fearfulness or pain is interpreted by him as "She doesn't want me when I'm afraid." Maybe it is even received as "Mommie doesn't love me." The injury or fearfulness is thus magnified with feelings of rejection, shame or guilt.

The womb was a warm, cozy place—the perfect protection from harm. Returning to the fetal position when we are asleep, cold or afraid acknowledges the imprint of the womb experience. So, a *gradual* movement away from this paradise must be provided by the touching and warmth of parents, primarily, and by other loving adults. Sudden or prolonged isolation from physical contact can be traumatic and will certainly not program a child with basic feelings of security.

Communicating with the Young Child

The child from one to five or six is like a sponge, soaking up a lifetime of opinions and biases. Virtually all of the basic attitudes about life are formed before the age of five. Among these ideas and biases is the picture of self which the child develops and lives up to for his or her entire life. This has to be regarded as the most important time of all for parents to communicate the constructive concepts upon which this new life will be built.

This is the time when father must be strongly evident. It would be a mistake for the male parent to wait for the children to get "old enough" for him to play a major role. Both parents must be with the children as much as possible at mealtime, bedtime and playtime. Parents should let children be with them as much as possible to observe male and female roles. Mother and Dad should take turns bathing the children, getting them ready for bed and taking them to the bathroom during the night.

Bedtime should be made particularly pleasurable—going to bed must NEVER be a punishment. Mother and Dad should tell quiet, relaxing bedtime stories or sing little songs as the children settle down, getting ready for sleep. Children will sense the pleasure of reading (some will even want to "read" pictures to their parents) and, most important of all, will sense the sincere interest which their parents have in them. It is a time to talk and to listen to concerns expressed by young, impressionable minds. It is a time to pass on family traditions and to build anticipation for future events.

Older brothers and sisters should participate with parents in bedtime activities consistently, rather than on rare occasions. As a matter of fact, babysitters can learn how to participate in these nightly rituals so that bedtime continues to be a happy time even when Mom and Dad need to go out for the evening. It must be recognized, though, that sitters can never really substitute for family members, no matter how carefully they are chosen. The fears and concerns of kindergartners and first graders will come forth while getting ready for bed, so all who work with these young children should be very good listeners, parents particularly, so the fears can be allayed.

Young children interpret our words quite literally—prereaders especially—as in the case of the second grader, a budding artist, who was asked by his teacher to draw a Christmas scene. He seemed to be taking great pains with his work, so the teacher stopped by his desk to offer a few words of praise. To her amazement, she discovered he had drawn two large people, one medium-size person and a small child—in an airplane!

"Tell me about your picture, Joe," she said, so he pointed out the figures.

"This is Joseph; this one is Mary, the mother; and this is the baby Jesus," he told her. "They're running away in an airplane from the bad king."

"That is a beautiful picture," said the teacher, "but who is the other person? He looks like he's flying the plane."

"Oh, he is, Mrs. Davis. That's Pontius, the pilot."

Other prereaders have been known to learn songs from their parents and then draw pictures of such things as "Round John Virgin" and "The Constipated Cross-eyed Bear."

What it all boils down to is this: Children believe everything they think they hear. So, it behooves parents to take extra care in listening and in speaking.

Many families use their own childhood prayers to teach their little ones, almost before they can utter full sentences and, sometimes, the phrasing can be frightening. "If I should die before I wake" could prevent a bright youngster from wanting to go to bed or, at the very least, fill his immature understanding with great concern.

Another required nightly ritual should be toilet time—just before bed and again at the parents' bedtime. Many preschoolers can be taken to the bathroom by their parents and literally be asleep during the entire routine. Others may have no problem connected with bladder capacity, but parents who take their little ones to the toilet every night will have more restful little sleepers and fewer problems in the morning. Bedwetting should never be looked upon as a shameful deed, though. Children sleep so soundly that some of them, snug and cozy in their warm covers, wake up only enough to dream that they are already in the bathroom. Cutting down on liquids just before bed and the nightly ritual at parents' bedtime will alleviate the bedwetting syndrome for the average youngster.

Preadolescent Family Communication

The period during the later elementary-school years is the time when children feel the first urges for independence. Although feelings are not yet strong, the "fourth-grade syndrome," well known to teachers, starts to be evident. This is the time when children no longer take everything adults say as gospel—they begin to question what they are told. This is quite normal and should be no cause for alarm. At the same time, it is a growth step to be recognized and accepted in the proper way.

Parents need to stay very close to children during this period. While beginning to express these independent feelings, ten to twelve-year-olds still need closeness. This means no cessation in touching, good-night kisses or time spent together. They should be allowed to work on chores with all family members, learning and contributing as they can. There should be time for informal, relaxed conversation and reading and singing together. Family planning for vacations and coming events provides exciting involvement for all family members and promotes unity, mutual respect and love. Parents should encourage contributions of ideas and suggestions about family activities. This will not diminish parental authority but, instead, will enhance the concept that the family is a very special team.

Adolescence: A Special Challenge

The most critical point in parent-child communication will usually come during the adolescent years. This is the time when bonds built during infancy and childhood will be tested as the child makes a major leap toward individuality in preparation for adult independence. If is often a period of turmoil and conflict because neither parent nor child understands the physical and mental changes which are occurring. It is imperative that parents understand the impulses which energize the child during this period of dramatic change and accept that as essential for healthy growth. It is natural, normal and of utmost necessity that children explore and experiment during this time and that parents provide a climate conducive to fulfilling these needs.

Children will push for as much freedom as possible, so parents must walk the thin line between "too much" and "not enough." This isn't easy, and parents may find themselves saying no more than their children would like, but reasonable boundaries are necessary and will be appreciated by a child eventually, even though resented at the time. "Dad (or Mom) won't let me" can be a good buffer against peer pressure which could overcome a youngster's uncertain conscience. Parents have to settle for long-term appreciation at the sacrifice of short-term gratitude from adolescents.

Reinforcement of parental love is particularly crucial during this period of "pulling away" by children. Touching and hugging must continue even though there is some resistance, and the phrase "I love you" needs repeating by parents. It needs to be extracted from children in return, too, to make it an habitual exchange. Fortunately, affection comes easier later if the loving is never stopped. Gentle firmness and stability are needs of adolescents whether they acknowledge it or not. Any inconsistency or division of parents will be readily exploited, so it is not a time for equivocation.

Communication with Adult Offspring

The continued closeness of parents and adult offspring can be the most rewarding aspect of the relationship if parents have done a good job and if they love their children enough to give them up. They are now capable of caring for themselves and making decisions independently, with only minor help from their primary home. Contacts gradually become less frequent as children go off to college or leave home to make careers for themselves. But love does not wane; so when they do come home, feelings may even be greatly intensified. Periods at home become "events" to be anticipated and relished.

Parents must permit their mature offspring to be truly self-reliant. To overprotect, dote upon or meddle in the affairs of the mature, independent son or daughter is unwise. This is not to say that help cannot be given in rough times, but this should be the exception; maturity comes in steps as challenges are faced and overcome. Interest in their accomplishments will always be in order, but interest in their problems should be avoided. Acceptance of *their* choice of mate, lifestyle and place of living is mandatory. If the values imbued during childhood do not produce choices which harmonize with those of the parents, it is too late to do anything but accept them without criticism.

Parents should show pride by tastefully displaying their children's pictures and retaining mementos of childhood. If parents still live in the house where the children grew up, it is well to refer to the children's previous bedrooms as theirs—no matter what use is now made of them. Mature offspring should be encouraged to visit when they want but not encouraged to run home when they have had conflict with their spouses. Parents should visit children's homes enough to show interest but not enough to become burdens. The new family needs room to breathe and develop in preparation for the next generation.

SUMMARY CHECK LIST

1. Communicate love and acceptance at all ages.

2. Emphasize praise above negative criticism.

3. Be sensitive to "message received" rather than "message sent."

4. Choose proper times to communicate.

5. Stress cuddling of infants by both parents.

6. Involve small children in family discussions and planning of events.

7. Alternate between parents the responsibility of putting children to bed.

8. Have meals together as a family.

9. Make bedtime a pleasant time.

10. Recognize adolescence as a special time for communication.

11. Supplement oral communication with touching, holding, kissing, etc., at all ages.

12. Give gentle firmness, the expression of true parental love, to teenagers.

13. Accept the reality of the children's leaving home and give them their independence. Relish in their maturity.

14. Maintain intense but infrequent contacts with adult offspring.

15. Don't meddle in the personal affairs of adult offspring.

Chapter 6

TEACHING HAPPINESS

Some wise person once remarked that the reason so many people do not find happiness is because the things that bring true happiness do not cost anything. This is an oversimplification, but it does suggest an important clue to happy living — appreciation for the simple things which are all around us. One who is not sensitive to the beauty of the world because of his preoccupation with other concerns is not as well off as someone who is blind. Is there any way to describe the exhilaration we get from beautiful music, a breathtaking sunset or a kind word of praise? Yet these are not commonly the targets of our striving for happiness. Too many lives are like that of the man who, when he finds he is running in the opposite direction from his destination, redoubles his efforts rather than turning around.

This is not intended to be a sermon about how our world has lost proper values or how foolish people can be; it is, however, an attempt to help adults realize —

1. how little attention is given to teaching children the causes of happiness;
2. that living patterns and goals in other areas can be compatible with happiness;
3. that happiness is not an end result but a process;
4. that happiness is an individual accomplishment, and the conditions which bring it about differ greatly among people.

Happiness Takes Conscious Planning

Every family, or certainly the family leaders, should periodically assess how the unit is doing in regard to happiness. Not only will this derive pleasure for all family members, but it is also teaching by example a skill to children which will help them in their young lives and later when they become parents. Fun activities and

37

happiness are synonymous to young children because immaturity demands short-term experiences. Happiness must be experienced in little bites at first and in larger (long-range) amounts as children grow.

This is true to the failproof theory because happiness is progressively learned, based upon abilities and needs correlated to maturity. Abstract sources of pleasure are introduced gradually as children grow; a choice of activity not correlated to maturity would fail as a happiness producer. Fortunately, much adult happiness stems from making children happy, so the needs of both generations dovetail well. Long-range happiness for adults often stems from providing short-range happiness experiences for children.

Conscious planning is the key. One family discovered that Sunday-evening singing around the piano was fun, so they built that into the weekly schedule. In another family, the father found that occasionally bringing home an assortment of candy bars and having family members draw blindly from a "grab bag" caused excitement. The anticipation of drawing an unknown candy bar for dessert was thrilling. Something less damaging to teeth should have been substituted but the concept is valid.

Still another family learned that constructing Christmas decorations and making gifts together was exciting. The anticipation started to build months before Christmas and thus became a long-term source of good feelings. Another spent weeks of enjoyment going over maps while planning for vacation. All of these activities, and many like them, are examples of how happiness can be "built into" ordinary living. It also would be well to note the cost of these activities: all are low in terms of money, but all involve sensitivity to what is important, including time commitments.

Happy Children — What Is Required of Parents?

Johnny had busy, financially successful parents. They bought him everything imaginable: toys, clothes, expensive trips to camp, and a new car the day he was sixteen. Unfortunately, Mom and Dad had little time for Johnny because they had to devote most of their time to maintaining a standard of living and earning the money to pay for their home and all the trappings of country club living. Johnny was the envy of all of his friends, who didn't know how unhappy he really was. He yearned for the attention of his parents and the security of their love but these were never given. He was unhappy, frustrated and psychologically crippled.

Jane came from a family of modest means. There were few toys and clothes, but the infrequency of new things made getting them exciting. Jane and her parents had to work together on family chores, and Jane had to be taught to do many things for herself. This meant much time with her parents as they labored together to meet their needs and the needs of the family's other children. Jane knew that nothing in the world was of higher priority to her parents than she, and the family love was obvious. Her lack of tangible things was more than compensated by the security of parental love.

These two stories illustrate how parental priorities can affect children. Indulging them with money is not nearly as productive as indulging them with love. Nothing compensates for the human contact; nothing makes up for lack of time together. There are no substitutes for intense parent-child relationships.

The Thrill Is in the Chase

A basic mistake made by many people is to assume that happiness is a point to be reached instead of a process of seeking. This attitude is instilled in young people, so they spend a lifetime trying to find *the* place or thing which brings happiness. A little thought and reflection quickly dispels that notion because happiness comes during the pursuit but diminishes quickly when the goal is reached if another goal is not chosen to fill the void.

This phenomenon is easily recognizable in people who retire only to find the leisure they sought so long is not enjoyable but an oppressing bore. Many people die of this boredom because their vocation, which provided meaning for their life, is gone. They were happy while working to achieve the goal of retirement; but when this was accomplished, there was no new goal—nothing to work toward—not even a reason to continue living. Psychologists now emphasize the importance of retiring *to* a new challenge rather than *from* a life's work—a crucial difference.

Robert Browning wrote: "Ah, but a man's reach should exceed his grasp,/Or what's a heaven for?" The excitement of pursuit, the thrill of the chase—these give the spice to life. Shakespeare talked about things being more exciting during the chase than after the capture. Both poets are reflecting upon this same theme which has much to say about the true nature of happiness.

We must have goals to stimulate us, we must set new goals periodically, and we must feel we can accomplish them ourselves.

Parents can rob their children of happiness if they do everything for them rather than merely giving them the stimulation, support and encouragement to do for themselves. Children need doors opened, the skills to be able to do, and an understanding of temporary setbacks—but no more. The welfare syndrome must be avoided: When people are given everything without efforts on their own, it destroys them.

Parents who have struggled to get where they are often make the mistake of denying children these same experiences. It is so easy and fulfilling for the parents to provide the things for children which they did not have themselves at a comparable stage of life. But this robs children of a chance to learn their own survival skills and to achieve their own feelings of accomplishment in life. Parents who overdo for children are salving their own egos at the expense of the children.

It may seem wrong when the son or daughter who has lived in a five-bedroom home earned by the parents must, upon marriage, move into a one-bedroom apartment; but it is not wrong. The newly-weds are beginning their own journey, which they must have the experience of making and enjoying in the process. This is the struggle they need to make together to appreciate the home they will eventually earn.

Happiness Is a State of Mind

A common error which is often made is to construct an image of what things or situations bring happiness, then impose these values upon others as if happiness had the same definition and dimensions for all people. The fallacy of this assumption is obvious when one considers that two people of similar age, intellect and physical ability find pleasure in completely opposite ways. One man may live in voluntary poverty as a missionary in a distant land while the other works on Wall Street as a wealthy stockbroker. Both can be happy in their chosen roles; but if the roles were reversed, they would each be miserable.

The important point for adults to realize is that a large element of personal choice is involved in happy living. Insisting that children pursue a particular career or lifestyle is usually unwise after the children are mature enough to know their own minds. Indoctrination while children are small is effective and advisable, but when they grow old enough to make independent decisions, the pressure should stop. A young person who wishes to pursue a career in the arts can be very unhappy as an executive in his or her parents' company, no matter what the salary.

Sources of True Happiness

Temporary good feeling which comes mainly from temporal pleasure does not provide long-term happiness. The parent who wishes to teach children how to acquire sustained happiness must realize this fact and look beyond the short term. This is not to say that an ice cream cone or a present is never to be given. These fit into the pattern of happy living, but ice cream cones are pleasures of temporary duration. The child must also be taught the sources of continued happiness.

While no system provides constant happiness, the goal is to tip the scales firmly in that direction. Another analogy might be the balance-sheet concept. Life has its ups and downs; this is natural. But it is possible to have the majority of life on the plus side by understanding the sources of enduring happiness. What are these sources? The list would differ somewhat depending on the individual; but for most people, the following would apply:

Conscience Needs

The values which are built into a child at a very young age tend to act as an inner judge throughout life. It is the voice within which tells us whether what we are doing is right for us. The same activity might be approved or disapproved by the consciences of different individuals, depending upon the programming of each conscience. For example, the child who was programmed so that going to church every Sunday is the right thing to do will probably not be happy in later life unless church attendance is continued. What some would call situational ethics is, for the most part, value judgments made within the framework of differing value systems.

Happiness for an extended period demands a contented conscience. This contentment will not come if the person's behavior is not in harmony with the values built into his mental computer. Much psychiatric treatment is simply an attempt to help a person live with his or her conscience; often, the adjustment can be made by the individual involved if he recognizes the source of his discomfort.

Socialization Needs

Most people feel a strong urge to be part of a social group, whether it is family, a club, church or, simply, acceptance in the school class.

Being without social contacts which make us feel accepted by other human beings causes discomfort; acceptance makes us feel good.

Children must be taught how to get along with others so they are accepted and do not become outcasts. They must be taught how to disagree without being disagreeable, how to maintain personal standards and principles without being social misfits. This takes skill learned from training and experience.

Often, recommended therapy for unhappiness is to become a member of a group. Counseling of depressed people is done primarily in group sessions because membership in the group is essential to the cure. Sharing our thoughts, concerns, victories and trivia with another person is necessary because of our socialization urges.

Accomplishment Needs

Feelings of self-worth are crucial to happiness. This is another way of saying *feelings of accomplishment* because self-worth stems from this source. Once again we are dealing with a relative term because the interpretation of what is an accomplishment varies greatly among people. Measures of accomplishment also vary—to one it is the accumulation of money while to another it is building a piece of furniture. The importance depends upon the values of the doer.

Parents should recognize that accomplishments do bring happiness, that there is no one achievement which brings it for all people, and that lack of the feeling causes unhappiness. This realization will cause parents to consciously teach the concept and provide opportunities for children to do things to experience that feeling. It will also keep parents from doing too much for children and robbing them of these experiences.

The unhappiest people are those who feel their lives do not count for anything. In other words, they feel a lack of accomplishment. Parents can see this phenomenon in miniature when children procrastinate. The period of leisure while tasks await is not a happy time. The good feelings come forth when the work is done. Indeed, leisure without prior accomplishment is deadly boredom.

The Christmas Morning Phenomenon

There is a lesson to be learned about maximum happiness by observing individuals as they open presents around the tree on Christmas morning. A family member will show excitement and happy anticipation as he opens a present. But observe that same individual when another family member opens a present which *he* gave! The happiness of the giver is greatest of all.

This lesson must not be overlooked as we search for maximum happiness and as we teach others to be successful seekers. Giving to others is a sure way of making ourselves feel good. This explains why people give to charity and do volunteer work. Certainly, the recipient is helped, but it also returns to the giver a feeling which is essential for his or her own well-being.

Some will make a career of work which is sacrificial from the standpoint of money earned. But the life which results can bring something which money cannot buy—happiness. Parents would do well to consider this as they build attitudes into children. What are the priorities when careers are chosen? Will money be given priority over happiness? If a career is chosen which brings money and happiness, this is fine; but if there must be a choice, happiness should be the deciding factor.

The Christmas Morning Phenomenon can also be used to make children happier while they are young. Activities which serve the needs of others should be included in childhood experiences. Collections for the needy, work with the handicapped, service to the elderly are examples of many opportunities which are available. The theory of "bread cast upon the waters" is scientifically valid.

The Danger of Possessions

Philosophers have written since the beginning of time about what happens to people who accumulate wealth and tangible items in their search for happiness. The Bible tells us "it is easier for a camel to go through the eye of a needle" than for a rich man to reach his goal of peace with his soul. It also tells of a man who accumulated storehouses full of possessions only to die before he could enjoy them. Thoreau writes of the farmers of Concord, Massachusetts, who worked for years to build elaborate homes and then found they were slaves to those homes. The lesson is clear—possessions can be a source of worry and unhappiness.

What, then, are we to do? Shall we live in perpetual poverty, never accumulating money because of fears about inflation? Shall we never buy a new car because someone may dent a fender? This view would be too extreme, but the opposite—becoming servants to our possessions—must also be avoided. Moderation in this, as in most situations, seems to be the best way.

Choice of things possessed is a key. A complete education should be valued over tangible things, a good reputation over a "money-by-any-means" attitude.

The road to possessions is another key. Denying oneself the pleasure of a close family relationship in order to acquire money is a poor decision. The feeling about the work we do is more important than the financial return.

There is no simple answer to the problem of possessions. The only realistic advice is for each person, each family, to constantly assess the situation. If happiness is being sacrificed in the striving for things, adjustments are in order. If pursuit of the tangible goal is not itself pleasurable, a change should be made. The vicious cycle of happiness-delayed while attaining a possession, and worry that it may be lost after it is attained, has been the pattern of too many lives. Ebenezer Scrooge found happiness only when he discovered how to overcome his possessions.

Socialization and Solitude

Successful living requires the ability to socialize—to get along with people at work and play. Much of the joy of life comes from human contact. The severest punishment which can be given a person is total isolation from others; solitary confinement in prison is the ultimate of harsh punishment. But the person who cannot survive without constant human contact is destined for unhappiness just as surely as the painfully shy person. The balanced life of socialization interspersed with periods of solitude produces the greatest potential for happiness.

An insatiable hunger for being with people is unnatural. Such a drive cannot be satisfied all the time; a person must learn to welcome occasional periods completely alone. As with all attitudes, this creative use of solitude must be learned. Activities which can be enjoyed by oneself are necessary, as is the habit of periodic meditation and contemplation.

Parents should encourage their child to spend time alone in his or her room reading, thinking, listening to music or playing games. In this way, his imagination has a chance to expand without evaluation of parents or peers. This retreat to collect one's thoughts and put life in perspective is a healthy mental refresher.

Balance is the key for socialization and solitude at any age. Excessive time spent in either is unhealthy. Parents need to teach and demonstrate in their own living the desired balance. The one-child family will probably need to provide for socialization because it is less likely to come naturally. Families with several children will need to ensure periods of privacy for individual children. Parents must also respect the right of children to have their privacy for periods of solitude just as they respect their right to reasonable privacy in all other areas.

The Tragic Ten-second Lapse

Scene I: Several teenagers have been laughing and indulging in horseplay as they walk down a neighborhood street. One spots an automobile with keys in the ignition. A dare, a momentary lapse of reasoning result in tragedy. It was just to be a joy ride in a "borrowed" car, but a friend dies in the accident. The driver has incurred a painful scar for life from the ten-second lapse of judgment.

Scene II: A group of college freshmen decides to play a trick on a friend by spiking his food with sleeping pills. The picture of him uncontrollably falling asleep in class sends his peers into gales of laughter. The fun turns to horror when he lapses into a coma and suffers brain damage.

The media constantly report the tragic ten-second lapse. The girl who dives into shallow water and is paralyzed for life, the boy who builds a homemade bomb and is blinded by the accidental explosion —the list goes on, though most incidents could be avoided by parents who supervise their children and who teach prevention of such incidents.

There is no way of knowing how many such tragedies have been prevented by parents who discuss with their children the concept of temporary lapses in judgment. It can be shown that, when such incidents occur, rarely have the children been prepared by such discussions with parents and other adults.

It is a topic which must be discussed and emphasized while children are young. Examples must be appropriate to the maturity of children to prevent scaring them unnecessarily, but children must be taught to think ahead, at all times, to the outcome of their actions. They must realize that a temporary error in judgment can cause a lifetime of regret and anguish. The tragic ten-second lapse always stems from an unwillingness to assess the possible consequences of a given action.

Compensate for Impediments

Any physical handicap or deviation in appearance can be a source of continuous embarrassment, so parents should make every possible effort to correct or minimize these. In some cases, impediments cannot be eliminated entirely, so psychological reinforcement is necessary to minimize the mental impact. It is heart-rending to see a child with a lingering physical abnormality which could be corrected by surgery or a child with extremely crooked teeth because orthodontic treatment has not been provided.

The timing of such treatment is also very important. A general rule is: the younger the better. The chance of psychological scarring is least when corrective action is taken at a very young age. Cross-eye, harelip, pronounced birthmarks and similar disfigurements can usually be repaired in infancy. Physicians should encourage early treatment, but parents should not hesitate to press them for the earliest time medically feasible.

Such corrections may cost a great deal of money and may require physical therapy over an extended period. It will be worth whatever it costs. A lifetime of pain versus the opportunity for happiness are the choices.

Marriage without Emotion

Admittedly, the selection of a mate cannot be made apart from emotion. The point is that marriage ceases to rest solely upon emotion at an early point in time, so such a momentous decision should at least include serious consideration of other factors. This kind of thinking must begin early in life and it must be initiated by parents.

The ideal selection of a marriage partner and co-parent would be a process which combines strong emotion and rational reasoning. It is not an unattainable ideal if this is the concept stressed early in life. Young people should be taught to judge their companions according to a check list of common interests so that a person selected for a casual date who does not fit the criteria will never even be thought of as a potential partner and co-parent. If the idea of stringent guidelines in selection of a husband or wife is always kept in mind, chances are good that a person not meeting the criteria will never be seriously considered. The fact that strong emotion and sexual drives will still prevail in some situations is no reason to capitulate.

Marriage is a long-term commitment even in this age of frequent and relatively easy divorce. The possibility for readjustment by the adults involved is not too difficult, but the real problem is with regard to the children. Once the obligation of parenthood is undertaken, it should not be vacated until the children are grown and prepared for independent living. They have a right to a preparation for life in a dual-parent home unless death intervenes. This mandates that marriage not be a selfish decision based upon the desires of the contracting parties. The subsequent issue of children is not present at the contracting ceremony but their fate is at stake.

The rights of potential children mandates a decision based upon more than emotion. What are these factors? A general guide is to have as many similarities as possible between the contracting parties. Anything which separates them philosophically is a potential source of irritation and conflict. These are the things which cause long-term problems after the emotional attraction has subsided.

The common elements are not hard to define: similar religious philosophies, common stands on political issues, agreement on leisure pursuits and lifestyles. Everything upon which there is agreement is a plus for the long term; every disagreement is a minus. Even minor differences must be considered because, while they do not loom ominously during the emotional phase, they will be very important in the long run. Minor differences "fester" and become incurable cancers with the passage of time.

The concept of marriage without emotion can be implemented in various ways. Parents can teach a child to develop a check list of items based upon his or her own preferences and use this as a guide when judging possible mates. The original attraction, which is entirely emotional, is then leveled by the unemotional evaluation. This balancing of emotion and practicality reduces the risk of a potentially unhappy life for the contracting parties and, even more important, for the next generation—which may experience a broken home or one that is in conflict.

Decide To Be Happy

Studies of successful people and how they achieved success always reveal this common finding: successful people decided to be successful and did whatever was necessary to make it happen. The same approach can be used in achieving happiness. The first step is to identify what it is for a given individual and then to do what is necessary to fulfill these requirements.

This may sound very simple to do, but in reality it is not. It could mean a change of vocations, divorce, or some other drastic adjustment in lifestyle. Obviously, the earlier in life a person can know himself, the sooner educational, job-selection and other large decisions can be made which reflect the essential elements for happiness.

Children must be taught that they must not permit themselves to fall into traditional traps of erroneous thinking, such as the idea that money and happiness are the same. Parents will need to guide them in how to plan for happiness based upon personal likes, abilities, traits and biases. Personal-happiness goals can be set and decisions made based upon those objectives. This type of analysis and wise planning prevents errors of omission and consciously keeps happiness in focus with other goals.

SUMMARY CHECK LIST

1. Recognize that real happiness always comes from simple sources.

2. Happiness is a process, not a reward or achievement.

3. Children must be taught what happiness really is and how to achieve it for themselves.

4. Happiness is an individual thing, so no one set of circumstances works for everyone.

5. Parents who indulge their children with money usually cause them long-term unhappiness.

6. Once a goal is accomplished, a new one must be set to maintain the "thrill of the chase."

7. A sense of personal accomplishment is essential for happiness.

8. Happiness requires a blend of social contacts and solitude.

9. A feeling of security and belonging helps achieve contentment and freedom from fear.

10. Doing for others brings more happiness than doing for self or having others do for you.

11. Possessions gained can bring worry over their loss or lack of utilization.

12. Long-term unhappiness can come from a very brief lapse of good judgment.

13. Handicaps need to be overcome, corrected or compensated for in order to minimize the threat to the best possible self-image and feelings of adequacy.

14. Marriage should be as rational a decision as possible because bad marriages bring great unhappiness for parents and, more importantly, for the children.

15. Being happy requires a conscious decision to do so and the action to make it a reality.

Chapter 7

DISCIPLINE AND PUNISHMENT

The two principal words in the title of this chapter are often used interchangeably to describe actions taken to correct behavior of children. In the vocabularies of many parents and teachers, both mean the same thing—punishment. In this discussion, a distinction will be made between the two: discipline will be the program of experience undertaken to prepare a child for independence, while punishment will concern corrective actions which must be taken when the child violates desirable rules of behavior or when he fails to exercise self-control. The differentiation is important because discipline (self-control) requires more than just punishment to be successful; a systematic program of teaching and learning is essential if a child is to master himself in our complex world. Discipline is the major goal and punishment only a *small* part occasionally necessary for attaining the goal. All education should be directed toward increased independence on the part of the learner until the ultimate in total independence is achieved. Homes and schools should operate in such a way as to give increased freedom and independence in increments as the child grows.

The failproofing approach of gradual progress, in keeping with ability and past experience, is just as valid in teaching discipline as anything else. Each month and each year should find the young person more responsible for meeting obligations and doing other tasks which demonstrate greater self-control. This program must move ahead constantly, which requires conscious planning by parents and teachers and self-constraint on the part of adults.

The Smothering Instinct

There seems to be a natural drive by parents to make all decisions for children. This has a crippling effect because it denies young ones the opportunity to gain maximum experience in decision making and living with the results. It is important to mention at this juncture that it is not proposed that children suffer injury while parents stand by as observers; this is taking the idea to an extreme. The proposal, instead, is to avoid the other extreme of making decisions which are within the ability of the child. Parents must fight the urge to smother children. Any time an adult makes a decision which the child could have made has, in effect, denied him an important growth experience.

Many examples could be offered to show the growth in independence and self-discipline which is achieved when parents overcome the urge to make all decisions; this is but one: A ten-year-old is given a certain amount of money each week for spending on entertainment items such as candy, movies and similar incidentals. On Tuesday he decides, on impulse, to buy a dozen comic books. The parents do not overrule the purchase but they do remind him that his allowance for the week will be exhausted. He goes ahead and makes the purchase; then on Saturday, he decides to go to a movie with a friend. The parents do not give him extra money but explain that the movie trip will need to be postponed until next week.

Making choices and assuming responsibility for them are vital characteristics that need to be learned in the development of a mature adult. The parents could see what might happen, but they did not intercede by denying their son this needed learning experience. They did not say, "I told you so," or try to make the child feel guilty. Instead, they explained, reassuringly, that a movie would be possible very soon; and they helped the boy feel better, not worse, about the decision. The point is made even better when parents remain supportive.

Teaching, Not Preaching

We teach far more by example than by what we say; in fact, very little teaching occurs in the realm of attitude by talking. We can *tell* our children to obey the law, but we are *teaching* when they see us drive fifty in a thirty-mile-per-hour zone. We can *talk* of the harmful effects of smoking, but we *teach* when we smoke. We can *talk* about the importance of goals in life, but we *teach* as children watch how we set and pursue our goals. The examples that children see are what they copy.

Perhaps even more important is the psychological confusion which results from conflict between what is "preached" and what is lived. This confusion causes uncertainty and requires young people to grapple with a situation which is beyond their ability to interpret.

How, then, do we handle our weaknesses so that children are not confused and so they can grow and do better than we have done? Probably the best way is to live the best example that we can, and when this is less than we would like it to be, acknowledge it and express a hope and confidence in the children that they will come closer to achieving the goal. It is useless to make excuses, to lie and, much worse, to be a hypocrite!

Developing an Organized Lifestyle

The disciplined life is one where a person obeys the laws of man and nature and meets deadlines and similar obligations. This requires a habit of planning, orderliness in personal living and positive habits. Activities which produce these outcomes must be taught sequentially as children are ready to understand the teaching. These attributes do not develop spontaneously.

Once again, example is the best teaching method. If parents are orderly in their habits, if they are punctual and adhere to deadlines, the children will want to be that way. The reverse is also true: parents who are slovenly in their personal habits, who consistently oversleep or show up late for appointments, or who make excuses for unfinished work are teaching their children that these are normal forms of behavior.

In addition to setting a good example, teaching the organized lifestyle should include explanation and instruction. Since it will be as important to the young child as it will be when he is grown, he will need to be shown the secrets of mastering these skills. Motivational techniques described in an earlier chapter should be used for reinforcement. The explanation should not be a boastful one of parent accomplishments, but a matter-of-fact explanation of how simple planning is done and how things can be kept in an orderly fashion. For instance, he can learn that his room stays clean and orderly if he never lets the clutter get out of control through procrastination. A little straightening each day prevents the need for major projects.

Physical or Psychological Punishment?

The controversy of physical versus psychological punishment rages unabated after centuries. Probably, the answer to the dilemma is to use whatever is effective at each particular age of the child. Spanking a very young child will produce the desired results, but discussion, chastisement and withholding of privileges are most successful with adolescents and older youth. Physical punishment should be no more severe than necessary to make the point and *it must never be administered while the parent is angry*. The goal is to correct behavior and help the child grow. The goal must *not* be emotional release for the parent.

When a preadolescent child misbehaves, the first corrective action should be to call it to his attention without emotion. A second warning may be necessary, or even a third, depending upon the time between acts or the type of misbehavior. The parents should also try to determine the reason for the offending acts and try to remove the cause. For example, temptations may be too readily available and one corrective action might be to remove the temptation from the child (or the child from it).

If the misbehavior continues after these actions are taken, spanking on the posterior (with the hand only) is then justified, but preliminary actions must be taken. The parent should calmly remove the child from other people to a secluded place, such as another room. After saying something like, "Daddy loves you and doesn't want you to do that again; he's going to spank you so that you will remember," then the punishment should be carried out, gently, and should be followed by reassurance—such as with a hug and a smile. The object is to complete the action quickly and give him a feeling that his debt is now paid and he can make a fresh start. This use of physical punishment is preferable to psychological stress, which comes from lingering disapproval or withholding of affection. Reasonable spanking is less damaging in the long run.

The same is true in withholding privileges from the older child. An explanation given in private followed by the punishment as promised and a "return to grace" as soon as possible—these are the steps which accomplish the goal with the least danger of undesirable side effects.

Some children become sensitized by guilt-producing emotions induced by their parents. In other words, when parents consistently use angry criticism in an attempt to correct children's behavior, they may be creating side effects which will produce guilt-ridden, fearful, unproductive adults. Each time he is rebuked, the child becomes a little more sensitive, a little more susceptible. Taking advantage of this increasingly acute sense of shame by scolding him at every turn is certainly an effective way to keep him in line. Unfortunately, it can also produce a neurotic individual because it is so destructive to his self-image. An insidious form of child abuse, it obviously has no place in the failproof method of rearing children.

School Punishment

The concepts used in constructive punishment at home also apply at school. Easily understood actions which are of shortest possible duration are best. Moderate corporal punishment or extra duties served to repay damages done are preferable to actions which demean or unduly embarrass. Dunce caps and standing in the classroom corner violate the principle of punishment in private—not to mention their being cruel and medieval forms of torture. Suspension from school causes work to be missed (like putting a debtor in prison) and could hardly be considered positive. While suspension may be necessary in extreme cases, it would be better to keep the child in school, if at all possible. "On-campus suspension" is an idea with merit. This procedure requires a student to come to school for supervised study even when participation in regular classes is not permitted.

As in all punishment situations, counseling and psychological reinforcement should precede the action. Young people can pay their debts and keep growing best when a loving adult punishes positively with no intent of revenge. The adult should be as emotionally detached from the situation as possible.

Success Rewards versus Failure Punishments

To the maximum extent possible, emphasis should be on rewards for success. Every time a person is "caught" doing right, the chances are good the behavior will be repeated. Getting caught doing wrong appears to bring forth a similar repetition of behavior. Some experimental programs have been designed around this phenomenon and, in these schools, credit is given for accomplishment only; for example, students are marked present but not absent. Each day the child attends is counted toward the number necessary to complete a course of study. When absent, the child gets no credit.

This unusual approach is being used with children with special needs, but there is no reason to doubt the idea could be adapted to provide positive reinforcement for normal children. One way might be to give credit to course completion for work done as quickly or as slowly as the student is willing to work, thus keeping the emphasis on achievement only.

SUMMARY CHECK LIST

1. Differentiate between programs of discipline and punishment — make them two separate programs.

2. Overcome the smothering instinct.

3. Emphasize positive teaching instead of preaching.

4. Teach by example the organized lifestyle.

5. Use reasonable physical punishment instead of psychological punishment with young children.

6. Counsel before punishing.

7. Never punish while angry.

8. Punish in private.

9. Emphasize reward over compulsion, threat and negativism.

10. Be quick and constant with praise.

Chapter 8

REINFORCING CONSTRUCTIVE HABITS

A negative connotation generally accompanies the word *habit*. It should not because *positive* habits are useful tools which serve people of all ages. Negative habits have the reverse effect, so the challenge, then, becomes development of good habits and the prevention or elimination of bad habits. On the one hand, adults must give conscious consideration to the formation of habits in young people so that proper ones are instilled at the appropriate times; on the other hand, bad habits must be recognized so something can be done before they become ingrained.

In this area, an "ounce of prevention" is far superior to "a pound of cure." A good example has to do with smoking: if this habit is never begun, there is no craving; once addiction occurs, it is extremely difficult to overcome. This is a serious habit; minor patterns of behavior which do not involve physical addiction would not be as hard to correct, but the concept is the same and the comparison is valid.

A discussion of all habits, large and small, good and bad, would go far beyond the space available here. Some of the more important ones are discussed as illustrations. The failproof concept of progression can be used to develop positive habits and overcome negative ones.

The Organized Lifestyle as a Habit

Some people live a crisis-oriented life, moving from one major problem to another. This can be recognized in adults who hold similar jobs; one experiences crisis after crisis while another does the same job in an orderly way with little or no stress and tension. The difference is usually the operating lifestyle which has been assumed by these persons. Life is very much a self-fulfilling prophecy. If we plan and organize to deal with life, the world will respond to that cue. The person who is crisis oriented also finds that particular attitude is reflected by others with whom he comes in contact.

Children should be taught by precept and example simple skills of planning and organizing in all things large and small. They should be taught to set and meet deadlines to overcome procrastination and to value the precious resource called *time*. Life is easier and there is less conflict and frustration when the organized lifestyle becomes a habit.

When children are very young, they must be taught orderliness in caring for their possessions. "A place for everything and everything in its place" is a sound motto. Youngsters also need to be taught to plan the day by looking ahead and providing time for things which must be done. It means punctuality rather than tardiness, work before play and responsibility to keep commitments. This does not mean a harsh regimen; these attitudes can be taught to be practiced in a very relaxed way. The adoption of a comfortably planned life prevents rushing, haste and the criticism which inevitably results when obligations are not met.

The organized lifestyle requires rising in the morning early enough to prevent rushing to meet the day's obligations. A stress-filled day often begins by lack of discipline in getting up and getting started. Obligations must be anticipated and time set aside to do them. Scheduling of activities should be done routinely and the habit supported by sufficient self-discipline to prevent procrastination.

Parents first set a good example for little ones. As the child grows, he or she is encouraged to take the responsibility for his or her own planning and organizing. Little formal instruction will need to be done when the parental example is strong and when praise and obvious approval are given to the child for positive behavior. If mother and infant automatically pick up and put away toys after play, this will continue as the child grows, with the mother gradually reducing her participation. Mother never ceases her praise and approval, however; this must be given without fail every time the child evidences a behavior which the parent wants repeated.

Positive Health Habits

As with all learned behavior, patterns are developed at a very early age. For example, Americans generally consume far more salt than is healthy because the taste for salt is developed during childhood. It is hard for adults to adjust to drinking milk with a low butter-fat content because skim milk tastes watery compared to the whole milk they grew up drinking.

Fat babies are admired as robust and healthy when, in reality, many are developing tastes which will cause them to become fat adults. A better way is to build in children habits of taste which will promote good health. Diets low in sodium, fat and sugar will prevent the development of tastes which prefer many unwholesome foods. Parents should taste food before asking for the salt shaker. Babies should begin drinking low-fat milk as soon as the family physician or pediatrician gives his or her permission. Sugary cereals, soft drinks and candy should be avoided in favor of fruit, fruit juices and raw vegetables. Children who are rewarded with oranges or given apples as treats will continue to desire these wholesome foods later in life. One only need hear an adult reared in humble circumstances yearn for "cornbread and redeye gravy" to realize that eating tastes are indeed learned; today's preference for "junk foods" is learned in the same way.

Parents who intensely dislike particular foods, especially those which are considered essential to a healthy child's diet, should keep their opinions to themselves when those foods must occasionally be served. In this way, children will keep an open mind in the sampling of different foods. Of course, they can still be allowed to forego one specific dish—a privilege everyone ought to have.

Trips to the physician and dentist should be routine—without equivocation. That is something we must all do, habitually and without fail. Periodic checkups as preventive measures will mean that some visits, perhaps most, can be made without being shot up with hypodermic needles or having teeth ground by dental drills. Parents can make a big event out of the three-year-old's first trip to the dentist so the two can be introduced and the little one can proudly show how well he has "been brushing." Conscientious mothers will have been regularly taking their children to the pediatrician or family physician since the initial neonatal exam. These checkups are vital so that all immunizations are given and the dates recorded faithfully in the child's very own record book. Some states have space provided on the back of birth certificates where physicians or parents can add such information; families who move frequently will find that invaluable when a child starts school.

There will be times when visits to the dentist or doctor mean that some pain will be experienced. Putting off the trip to avoid pain is obviously not the answer. Explanations that "it won't hurt" only underscore the word *hurt* and bring a realization that the parents cannot be trusted to tell the truth. No matter how much parents would like to prevent all pain and unpleasantness, it is just not possible. Learning to accept reality is a growth step. The presence of loving parents will support a child; he will feel the hurt but be secure in the knowledge that his parents would not allow him to be harmed.

Tobacco, Alcohol and Drugs

Children copy behavior readily, but learning through interpretation of words is most inefficient. The parent who yells at his child is teaching him to yell, no matter what subject he may be on at the time. The behavior of adults with relation to smoking, drinking and drug usage is the strongest possible teaching. Children emulate this behavior in spite of what they are told about the consequences of such habits. If parents wish to take the strongest action to prevent children from using these substances, they will not indulge themselves.

What if parents do smoke or drink? Is it then impossible to prevent children from adopting such practices? The only reasonable answer is that it is not impossible but it is much more difficult. If hypocrisy is avoided completely, and if parents acknowledge that they wish they did not have these habits, children may understand and choose not to yield to the temptation.

Complete honesty is the only way to handle this situation. The parent who smokes and admits addiction can use himself or herself as an example of how someone can get hooked. The parent who drinks in moderation can openly teach the responsibility that goes with moderation. The confusion occurs when the parent attempts to rationalize the action or when a person tries to justify use of these substances rather than admit them as a weakness. Use of tobacco, alcohol and drugs occurs because of a felt need on the part of the user. Young people must be taught to fill their needs in wholesome ways so they will not use these "crutches."

Programs to prevent drug usage reflect this enlightened outlook and illustrate the point. The first programs tried to scare youngsters so they would avoid drugs. Jail inmates would describe the terrors of drug addiction and the horrors they had experienced; this approach failed miserably. The next phase emphasized understanding the effects of drugs, but this only increased interest and usage. The current approach, and by far the most effective, teaches young people to understand themselves, their needs and concerns so they can meet the needs in ways which build up rather than tear down. The use of "crutches" is a symptom rather than a cause. Dealing with and solving the cause is the most effective solution.

Use of Leisure-time Habits

The way leisure time is used can either contribute to a happy and successful life or be neutral, perhaps harmful. Leisure-time usage must not be overlooked as children are programmed for life. In the true sense of the word, some time is needed when a person is free to do what pleases him, but many children have far too many idle hours, particularly in summer. They fall into deadly bad habits, such as chronic television watching, which lead to boredom, self-depreciation and a lowered self-image. Parents must help children develop good use of leisure while avoiding overcommitment by pushing them into too many activities. The happy medium is a sensible goal because children who are pleasantly occupied with neither too much time on their hands nor too many obligations are the happiest.

When children watch too much television, they are living vicariously by watching other people do exciting things. Ultimately, they will be happier when they do the exciting things themselves and experience the excitement firsthand. The thrill of reading, of participating in hobbies and individual sports will contribute to growth while providing pleasure simultaneously. These interests do not develop spontaneously but require the leadership, motivation and good example of parents. Leisure pursuits must be taught with attention given to the maturity level of the learner. In other words, conscious attention must be given to the choice of tasks so the learner will experience success and satisfaction, not frustration.

For a well-rounded person, the choice of a variety of leisure pursuits is important. Individual sports are essential and contribute to good habits of health and personal hygiene. Participating only in sports, though, would leave much of the individual underdeveloped, particularly in the intellectual realm. A blend of leisure activities such as reading, music, hobbies and sports provides for a balanced development.

Microcosmic Adulthood

In many respects, childhood is a microcosm of adulthood. On a small scale, the patterns of behavior, taste and interest are being practiced and reinforced, developing the characteristics of a lifetime. The failproof concept requires that these patterns be positive and progressively increased, always pulling the learner toward success and growth but never to the point of frustration. Children are born winners; they will not fail unless adults fail in providing appropriate tasks and motivation.

SUMMARY CHECK LIST

1. Use habits to make constructive behavior automatic.

2. Recognize bad habits and take corrective measures early.

3. Teach primarily by example.

4. Emphasize the organized lifestyle.

5. Provide diets and health practices which are supportive throughout life.

6. Prevent children from smoking and drinking by using techniques that work.

7. Give attention to development of leisure activities that build.

Chapter 9

CRISIS-INCIDENTS

Under the failproof theory, whenever a child gets into trouble, it is the fault of the parents or other responsible adults. The child has encountered a challenge or temptation beyond his ability to cope without being overcome. If sufficient training had been done prior to the temptation, he would not have succumbed (see Chapter 7). The concept further emphasizes that a challenge must not be faced unless it can be conquered, based upon the actual training plus experience and attitude development. The shift of blame is at the heart of the failproofing approach.

The failproofing theory is just what the name implies; the extent to which it succeeds depends on one's ability to implement it to the fullest. It is not unrealistic to assume that there will be setbacks, and among these will be "crisis-incidents" of considerable magnitude. What happens then? Do we abandon our theory and give up being positive in favor of negativism, restraint and withdrawal? Definitely not. Using the positiveness of failproofing, we can turn the crisis into as minor an incident as possible, making it only a slight setback on the road to overall success. Of all the child-rearing methods, failproofing has the greatest potential for minimizing the impact of the crisis-incident.

What Are Crisis-Incidents?

There are all kinds of situations which would be considered as critical points in the life of a family. Here are a few:

Enjoying a quiet Sunday afternoon, a mother and father are sitting on the patio, reading the paper and casually discussing today's sermon by their pastor. The children are elsewhere in the neighborhood, playing with other young children. The telephone rings and, answering it, the father hears the voice of a distraught neighbor: "Your son was playing with matches in my basement and just about burned the house down—I've got to take my Bobby to the doctor—then I've got to come back here and figure out how much it's going to cost to replace the burned chair—what kind of a kid do you have, anyway?"

In another family, the mother is catching up on her household chores after an activity-filled weekend. She is drying her hands as she picks up the ringing telephone with little thought of what trauma she is about to encounter. The school counselor wants her and her husband to come to school as soon as possible. Their daughter has been privately carrying a great burden which finally got the best of her. The parents' fears are justified: their sixteen-year-old is pregnant.

A high school football player and honor student is arrested for using marijuana; a seventh-grade girl takes a bottle of liquor from the family supply and gets drunk at school; a student is caught cheating on a test and failed for the semester—these are typical crisis-incidents which can happen in any family.

Obviously, it would be well if crisis-incidents never occurred, but statistics show they usually do at some time in everyone's life. Although they may vary in severity, rare is the person who does not experience one or more while growing up. In some cases, largely due to the way adults handle them, crisis-incidents are repeated with ever-increasing frequency until that type of behavior becomes a way of life. Actions taken in the early stages make the difference between an isolated case in an otherwise successful life and a pattern of negative behavior leading to self-destruction. Juvenile delinquency is the generic term given to the behavior which produces chronic crisis-incidents. It is the positive approach inherent in failproofing which can be used to correct an isolated incident and prevent repetition of such crises.

Keep the Incident in Perspective

The first actions taken when a crisis-incident occurs are extremely important. There is a great tendency to overreact, to make the situation worse so that reconstructing it is difficult, if not impossible. The child is looking to the adult for clues as to how serious the incident really is and what ramifications it has created. Although the incident cannot be unduly minimized, or "shrugged off," the aim is to maintain perspective. The child needs his parents now more than ever; he does not need someone to put the fire out with kerosene!

Admittedly, it is difficult to maintain composure in a crisis which involves a loved one, but it is crucial. Perhaps the approach with most chance of success is to take the long view of life. How important will this episode be in five years, in ten or twenty? How does the episode look on the balance sheet of behavior? The reason it stands out is probably because behavior has been good up to this point. Should this not be taken into consideration? Perspective enables us to take these critical junctures and average them out over a lifetime, which is the fair and most constructive thing to do.

Five Steps in Dealing with Crisis-Incidents

1. Be calm.

The young person is usually quite upset, at loose ends or possibly panicky. The adult who calmly pursues the facts from both the accuser and the accused becomes the symbol of stability around which all can gather to work on the problem. He will only succeed in making things worse if he loses control. This is not the time to be self-righteous, indignant or to protect one's own ego with a statement like, "How could you do such a thing?" Above all, do not tell him you are ashamed of him. It is equivalent to telling him he is not worthy of your love.

2. Reassure him.

This is the time the young person is in real need. Let him know he has an advocate who is going to help him as much as possible. This does not mean snap judgments of innocence or hasty attacks on the accuser. It means to show support. Depending upon the incident, he may have done "a dumb thing" or "a shameful thing," and you may feel very angry, but the child involved in a critical situation needs a loving parent to stand with him, to help him face the crisis.

3. Make all corrections possible and pay the penalty.

Once facts have been established, help the young person make restitution and pay a rightful penalty. Parents should not make the payment for him, but they should facilitate his paying. Assuming he has the high values of the family and this has been an isolated incident, the period of payment will probably be a painful one. Continued support, devoid of abuse, will aid in the recovery of his self-esteem.

4. Prevent future incidents.

Take constructive and proper steps, bearing in mind the failproof approach, to avoid repetition of the improper behavior.

5. Return to normalcy.

Put the incident behind as soon as possible by returning to the normal routine of activity. The longer the routine is broken, the harder this will be, but reestablishment of normalcy is crucial.

Skeletons in the Closet Are Normal

Discussion of the crisis-incident will undoubtedly occur from time to time in the future. Generally, they come at less frequent intervals as time passes, but they are normal and healthy; this is an important part of the catharsis necessary for overcoming failure. Compassionate listening by parents will be helpful, particularly as a means of also overcoming the guilt.

There is nothing very unusual about misbehavior; "All have sinned." The important point is to use the experience gained from it to grow in a positive direction rather than have such conduct become a pattern. Some people get caught, others do not, but all people share in the knowledge that everyone has done something for which he is ashamed. The offense may vary, but the experience is commonly shared.

This understanding is helpful in living with guilt. We are not alone in our situation; everybody has some sort of "skeleton in the closet," and other people are far more concerned with protecting their "skeletons" than discovering ours. We need not dwell on our shortcomings; we are free to move forward — unafraid.

Indiscriminate Confessions Are Not Helpful

At the time of the incident, and at intervals in the future, it is helpful to have a confidant with whom to discuss the feelings which accompany the offense. Parents who are understanding and supportive will build a lifetime of rapport by listening. Caution must be given, however. The good feeling which accompanies confession can be addictive; the young person can easily overdo it. There is nothing to be gained by indiscriminate confession.

Children must be guided in curtailing the circle of persons who know about the problem — the smaller the circle, the better. It would be a mistake to give the world a "stick" to wield over oneself; virtually all human beings grasp at a chance to cover their own shortcomings by exposing those of others. Knowing in one's heart that restitution and correction have been made is sufficient; nothing can be gained by broadcasting it. To put it bluntly, it is nobody else's business!

As a matter of fact, parents should not share their own past crisis-incidents with their children. Certainly they should admit to being less than perfect, but that is sufficient. To recall past incidents which would be better forgotten is painful enough but, more important, nothing is gained by tarnishing the "hero image" children have of their parents. Revealing these negative episodes with a younger generation is ignoring the "balance sheet of life" and the concept of failproofing. "To err is human, to forgive, divine." Is it not reasonable to forgive ourselves as well as others?

Self-image Is of Most Importance

There is a vast difference in the way individuals survive crisis-incidents. They are a threat to the self-image, not so much as a result of the magnitude of the incident but in the person's perception of that magnitude, which is why two people suffering the same setback can perceive it completely differently. Some suffer very little, while the self-images of others are badly damaged.

We function in life according to our individual assessment of self-esteem and of the reliance we have in our own capabilities. Therefore, it is crucial that we employ the steps to maintain a stout ego so as to sustain a sturdy feeling of adequacy. Our challenge is to diminish the impact as much as possible by remaining positive as we deal constructively with the crisis.

SUMMARY CHECK LIST

1. Put the incident in perspective of a total lifetime.

2. Be calm during the crisis.

3. Provide reassurance; this is not the end of the world.

4. Correct the behavior and let the youngster pay a reasonable penalty.

5. Return to normal activity as soon as possible.

6. Develop the idea that having "skeletons in the closet" is a normal condition.

7. Confine confessions to a minimum number of people.

8. Protect and rebuild damaged self-images.

Chapter 10

SEX IN PERSPECTIVE

The most powerful force affecting human beings is, without question, the sex drive with its many variations and manifestations. It virtually dominates the individual after adolescence; prior to this time, the individual is learning from adults who are, themselves, controlled by it.

To deny the domination of the sex drive is to delude ourselves. Our feelings of adequacy and our willingness to venture forth stem from our perception of ourselves as sexual beings. Our choices of clothes, cars, vocations, and lifestyles are heavily influenced by our pictures of ourselves and the degree of masculinity or femininity we see— either consciously or, more often, unconsciously.

The person who is not perplexed by the picture he has of himself tends to be freer to grow, to feel comfortable with life. Self-respect, self-confidence, a sense of competitiveness and a willingness to take risks are characteristics of a person who also has few sexual inhibitions. Guilt, shame, fear, poor performance, generally—and in the sexual act, specifically—are examples of poor psycho-sexual adjustment. Failproofing of any individual requires an excellent sexual adjustment.

As in other areas of human behavior, growth is possible and negative elements are not a problem as long as an individual feels comfortable with his own choices and the world's reaction to those choices. Successful people are found with all types of lifestyles; the *feeling* about the lifestyle is the crucial element.

Formal Teaching of Sex

It is necessary to teach young people to put their sexuality into a perspective which allows them to lead effective lives. The failproofing concept of teaching by example may not be as readily understood since greater effort must be given to teaching in a more subtle form, but the concept is still valid. The models which are provided will instill attitudes—good or bad. Negative feelings of guilt and self-consciousness will develop if imitated behaviors are subsequently criticized or shamed. For example, if a child is teased by parents for having a boy or girl friend, it conflicts with the knowledge that the parents themselves have sexual interests. Using terms like "puppy love" confuses the child who is experiencing a natural sexual attraction. A much more wholesome approach would be for parents to guide the child in understanding those feelings, to provide ways in which to express them in a socially acceptable manner and to regard them as a perfectly normal and happy part of life.

The goal is to prepare the learner to solve any problem which he or she faces but not to supply challenges beyond his ability to succeed. He will then be ready to deal with the sexual feelings which come with adolescence, and he will be able to deal with them without embarrassment and with the ability to control sexual urges. Using this same concept, a younger child will not be burdened with unnecessary information beyond what is needed at any given point of physical and emotional development.

Teaching Sexual Roles

When sex education is mentioned, one usually believes it to mean teaching about reproduction. It is, but it should be much more than this. It should also include everything a person needs to know to play a strong sex role in a social order which is strongly sex-oriented. It means not only the development of techniques for successful sexual performance but also the attitudes which provide for maximum enjoyment of sex. It should also mean prevention of any feelings which could diminish one's ability to develop to the fullest.

In our society, clearly defined sex roles are most accepted, thus giving the most promise of *contributing to* rather than *detracting from* maximum growth. Parents who are distinctly feminine or masculine give children easier models to emulate. Men can still perform tasks which are generally done by women and vice versa as long as children understand it is exceptional. Problems occur when the line becomes blurred. Children succeed best when they are certain as to which sex role they should play. This may seem unimportant until it is recalled how poorly feminine boys or masculine girls get along in school; this atypical behavior is a substantial handicap.

Fathers must be good masculine models and mothers good feminine ones. Additionally, both parents must spend time with the children so they can absorb the behaviors appropriate to both roles. Many of the models on television are not worthy examples nor, in some cases, are babysitters or nursery school personnel.

This thinking will cause problems for those who support a movement toward a unisexual society or for those who see sexual roles as sex stereotyping, which implies lack of choice because of sex. A person who is confident in his or her own sexuality is not confined but is truly free to explore new and different paths. The primary factor, though, is the security, so it requires a clear and satisfying sexual self-image.

Sexual Knowledge Must Come Early

An unhealthy aura of mystery exists when information about sex is not given at an early age. Children sense something abnormal when other questions are answered forthrightly but questions about sex cause nervous responses or evasion. These preposterous reactions may even be continued long after the child knows better. Young children trust their parents and hold them in high esteem. When the deception becomes apparent, as it must if lies have been told, no amount of justifying can make up for the deceit.

Wholesome growth and healthy attitudes demand an end to the mystery and deception. Information should be given matter-of-factly, as it is needed, and in an atmosphere which makes sexuality a normal part of living.

In earlier times, most of this country's children had an opportunity to learn about reproduction when each spring brought forth new calves, pigs and lambs. In the urban society of today, it is a little more difficult; but since a large majority of families have pets, children can be shown that a puppy or a kitten came out of its mother's body. In the human family, if a new baby is on its way, children can hear and feel its movements in Mommy's tummy.

It would amaze some adults if they realized how little attention is given to sex organs by small children. For this reason, parent and child taking a bath together can develop a wholesome attitude toward sexual similarities or differences. When the children reach five or six, it is then time for them to bathe alone or separately, according to sex. This change helps reinforce sex roles and is done, not because nakedness is "dirty," but as a society, we choose to do some things separately as we grow older because we want to respect each other's privacy.

Bathing together is one illustration of how sex education can occur quite naturally. Differences in organs of male and female have been revealed, sex has been given no unnatural glamour or connotation, sex roles have been reinforced and maturity has been recognized by the adjustment to individual bathing. Much is accomplished in a simple, but effective, way with no adverse side effects.

At the outset, proper terms should be used for parts of the body and all questions must be answered directly, simply and without fanfare. When the child asks where he came from, he should be told that he came from inside his mother. When more information is needed, it will be asked as long as he knows his questions are welcomed. It is also wise to anticipate some questions and casually raise the subject in advance. The important thing, though, is not to make an issue or call undue attention to the topic. Sex should be discussed just as other interesting topics are discussed. This means no "birds-and-bees" discussions and no stilted "special talks" about sex.

Homosexuality

Psychologists differ as to whether homosexuality is a normal condition. No attempt is made here to settle that question nor to speak disparagingly of homosexuals. The purpose of this presentation is to help adults prepare young people for success. In that context, homosexuality must be looked upon negatively because children with traditional sexual identities (which match their actual sex) will find success easier to attain. The goal, then, is to rear children in such a way as to avoid their becoming homosexual.

Children get most of their sexual cues from parents, and their attitudes are absorbed at a very young age. The best assurance of heterosexuality is to have strong models in parents so that children can adopt balanced patterns of behavior appropriate to both sexes. If a male child becomes a close companion to a female model, this pattern of behavior will seem the natural one to adopt. Also, if a child intensely dislikes a particular parent, that model can be rejected.

Causes of homosexuality are much more complex than this, and parents must be sensitive to deviant behavior which might indicate the beginnings of homosexual tendencies.

The best advice is to not panic if a boy likes to play with dolls or if a girl enjoys rough sports. The basic attitude is the most important consideration. If a pattern of behavior evolves which is contrary to the actual sex of the child, positive approaches must be taken. A child-behavior specialist can recommend a progression of steps based upon the failproof approach to modify the behavior, but the earlier the modification is done, the more chance there is for complete success.

Sex Education in Schools

A mistake which parents must not make is to depend upon public or private schools to do the job of sex education. There are a number of reasons why this is so: schools start too late, administrators and teachers are too timid and they mainly teach mechanical aspects.

The pressures put upon schools by parents who have diverse, often passionate, views effectively neutralize even the most well-meaning efforts of educators. In addition, few teachers are knowledgeable enough or sufficiently free of "hang-ups" themselves, making this source of little value at best and possibly harmful.

Topics relative to the reproductive process should be taught in a biological context along with other health topics, but the attitudes, which are the most important, will probably not be taught well, if at all. Parents must look to themselves for the education of their children in sex-related matters.

Because of the constraining factors, schools would be well-advised to teach about sex only as the topic is a part of other school courses. Certainly, it should not be a special or separate program. Most important of all is to refrain from putting sex in an unwholesome context by having combined programs such as "Sex, Alcohol and Drugs." Incredible as it may seem, this was the title of a lecture given in one Florida high school. Worse yet, boys and girls were taught separately, thus accentuating the problem.

Horror stories about sex education programs in schools abound without limit, and little would be gained by relating a great number. However, one other illustration is in order: One school taught about sex in a special unit on body functions. The subject matter dealt with eliminating the bladder, voiding the colon, menstruation and ejaculation. To consider sexuality in such a narrow way is to deny its centrality to all of life. To give such a completely distorted view of reproduction by putting it in a group with waste elimination is hardly a proper or elevating perspective.

Physicians and Preachers As Sex Educators

Sex education occurs gradually and continually as children grow and observe, not through short spurts of indoctrination. Misguided parents may look to periodic lectures from physicians or clergymen to do a job in a brief time but it cannot be handled in this way. Passing the buck to someone else is not the answer unless problems are extreme; even then, careful attention must be given to the qualifications of the person.

Physicians can explain the mechanics of sex but, generally, they have as many problems in the attitudinal realm as anyone else. Clergymen are bound by religious doctrines which narrow the scope of their listening to include moralizing. Moral teachings are fine if the client already has self-confidence and basic knowledge on which to superimpose these chosen values. Physicians and preachers can play a supporting role, but the major task of sex education must fall upon parents.

Teaching by Example

Parents must consciously decide, and then practice, the moral values and attitudes they wish children to have. The brain is by far the most important sex organ. The misinformation, feelings and attitudes stored there will determine sexual proficiency and enjoyment. It is rare that sexual dysfunction stems from physiological causes.

Most of the sexual problems experienced by adults stem from taboos, myths and incorrect information. The male-aggressor syndrome comes from a mistaken notion that men should be attackers while females must be passive. Some women are taught that the purpose of sex is procreation and that it is not for enjoyment as well. Some men and women believe that simultaneous orgasms must always be achieved or the sex act will not be successful. These are typical of attitudes which cause diminished enjoyment, even frigidity and impotence, when sex should be the most enjoyable part of adulthood.

Sexual attitudes displayed by mother and father toward each other will be remembered by children as appropriate for their own spouses. Parents who treat each other with respect, who show genuine concern for the physical and emotional needs of the other will see this kind of behavior carry over into the next generation. On the other hand, if adults use their respective sex roles to abuse one another, either physically or psychologically, their children will see this as normal.

A home environment where parents are comfortable with themselves, with each other and where children can ask questions and share concerns produces the most wholesome growth. Children will learn about sex one way or another. Prolonged ignorance is not an alternative because other children will share their knowledge (much of it incorrect) and physical urges within the child will induce exploration.

It is important to have an open atmosphere where children can express themselves freely and receive constructive feedback from adults. When children repeat crude sexual terms, parents should neither express shock nor should they chastise. Rather, they should explain the acceptable alternative word and tell why it will serve them better.

Children should be allowed, even encouraged, to be interested in the opposite sex and taught to behave in such a manner as to receive approval of society and not embarrass themselves. The way to achieve this is not to attack sex as something "dirty" but to put it in perspective as an exciting, pleasurable part of life.

SUMMARY CHECK LIST

1. Put sexual teaching in context with other facts about living.

2. Provide strong heterosexual models for children.

3. Teach sexual facts early in life.

4. Recognize and modify homosexual behavior.

5. Don't expect schools and churches to do the job of sex education.

6. Explain crude sexual terms without embarrassment.

7. Teach family values and attitudes; stress them by living them.

Chapter 11

SUCCESS IN SCHOOL

Most of a child's attitudes, including his self-image, have been substantially developed prior to entering kindergarten or first grade. This fact should not lead to the false assumption that school is not extremely important. Things which are done or not done can modify self-image to a considerable degree or even profoundly change basic attitudes. Such large degrees of change are unusual but they can happen.

Even if attitudes are not greatly affected, there is still the need of children to master skills of communication and computation as well as gathering facts needed in the future. Attitude is of greater importance, but better yet is to have positive attitudes supported while learning the cognitive skills necessary for success. Good schools give constant attention to both needs as they use the elements of the failproof concept to ensure maximum growth and happiness for learners.

Parents must support the school in its great challenge of educating children of a pluralistic society, and they must also selfishly monitor what is happening to their most precious obligation and opportunity—their children. It is not sufficient to send children off to school and to merely ask the occasional perfunctory question: "What did you do in school today?" No other person in the world, not even a teacher, will have the intense interest in children as will the parents. The job of parenting is nontransferable and nonassignable, even to teachers. It remains a full-time job until children become adults.

Choosing a School

Far more attention should be given to the choice of a community for school purposes than for any other reason. The kind of school the child attends makes a great difference and, thus, should be carefully considered. The choosing of a school would be easy if all were alike and all were adequate, but they are not.

Schools tend to reflect the clientele they serve. If the families in the school area have high aspirations, then this will be reflected in everything from programs provided to dollars spent per child. The newness of the building is not a sure measure because many established neighborhoods have had a long tradition of good education even though the school building is older, while some emerging subdivisions are in chaos because of rapid growth. The best generalization is to choose an established school and neighborhood where parents hold their school in high esteem and where, in large numbers, they are actively involved. Neighborhoods where families or school staff tend to be transient should be avoided.

The atmosphere of the school should be exciting but stress-free. Teachers and other staff members should be warm and approachable so that an atmosphere of love is evident. The program should be extensive to meet the varying needs of all youngsters, including the gifted and handicapped. Books and other materials should be plentiful, and the library should serve as a true learning center. Parents should be involved, not only in groups such as PTA, but also as teacher aides and room representatives. The building should be clean, cheerful, and large enough to accommodate the children without crowding.

Middle schools, junior high schools and senior high schools should meet these same criteria. Moreover, the graduates should have distinguished themselves in college and the working world. Programs of advanced study in academics such as third and fourth-year language, physics, chemistry and second-year biology should be available. A full range of vocational courses for boys and girls and a complete activity program are musts. The student activities should include a full range of athletics for boys and girls in junior and senior high school, but other activities should be equally supported.

The size of the school population is an important consideration. While there is no research to support the idea that small elementary classes produce more learning, large classes are generally a sign of lack of financial commitment on the part of school leaders and the community. It also increases the chance that special learning needs may be overlooked by the teachers.

High schools should be large enough to offer a complete educational program and include enough students to support advanced academic courses. Normally, this will mean a high school of at least 1500-1800 students. If a school gets much larger, opportunities for any given student are diminished because of too much competition. No matter how large the school, there can be only one newspaper editor, one valedictorian and one first-string quarterback. Many students who would get these experiences in a smaller school are denied them because of sheer numbers.

Harmony among educational leaders is also an important factor in choosing a school community. If political hacks are using the school board as a platform for their own selfish political ambitions, schools will be harmed. Teacher unions can get a strangle hold and siphon off resources from the students. It is best to choose a school system where professional educational leadership is strong and where board members are educational statesmen serving at a sacrifice to themselves for the benefit of young people.

Public or Private School?

For a normal child, a good public school provides everything which is needed for a substantial education. Parents often think a private elementary or secondary school is best because of its cost, but this is seldom true. Private schools are costly because they do not receive tax support. If parents paid for their childrens' education in public school, they would be amazed at how much it costs. Private schools vary so much in quality that it is difficult to generalize about them, but much investigation is in order before parents decide to put a child in a private institution.

Some private schools charge very high tuition and serve an exclusive, academically elite clientele. Some charge very high tuition and serve children who cannot adjust to public school because of behavior problems. If a private school is under consideration, the entrance requirements are the best guide, rather than cost or any other criterion. High grades and test scores for entrance indicate an academically oriented school where high standards of education are likely. Low entrance requirements, or no entrance requirements other than money, indicate the school serves misfits who have been problems in public school.

There are many private schools which thrive on frustrated parents who either have children who are in trouble in public school or ones who have been expelled from other schools. Such institutions offer little but false hope and seldom do anything constructive. A thorough investigation, including an extended visit, should be undertaken before attempting to enroll a child in a private school. A reputable school will welcome such precautionary measures.

Nursery School

Nursery schools have flourished in the United States in recent years, mainly due to changes in family structure and the increasing number of women in the national work force. Grandparents, who once were built-in baby sitters for working parents, rarely remain in the homes of their children today. The decrease of family members as baby sitters occurring simultaneously with economic pressures on families seeking middle-class status provided two strong reasons for establishing some place to "store" young children. Nursery schools with deceptively charming names became the holding pens for great numbers of children abandoned, at least temporarily, by their parents.

There are not many nursery schools that house professional staff or have adequate facilities to do a good job and, even if they did, this is not a good substitute for a supportive home during these formative years. The amount of touching, loving and individual attention needed by infants and very young children cannot be given in a group situation. The isolation from parents and the danger of exposure to other children with emotional problems add to the hazards. Only the severest of economic situations should cause a parent or parents to consider such placement of an offspring.

If nursery school cannot be avoided, the risks can be lessened by the choice of school and compensating measures taken by the parents. Bearing in mind that *no* nursery school is as good as a stable home, the parents who must take this action would be well advised to study the chosen school. The leadership staff should be professionally trained, and other workers should be, at the very least, warm and loving. Adequate space for indoor and outdoor play should be a prerequisite; but no matter how much space is available, very large schools should be avoided.

Beware of promises of accelerated learning. Nursery schools should have very relaxed environments where emphasis is upon happiness and fun rather than discipline or work. The higher the ratio of children to adults, the more authoritarian will be the controls and thus the greater risk to mental health of the youngsters. Generally, a pastoral setting, such as is found in many church-related nursery schools is best. Large commercial operations are usually the most dangerous.

Parents who must use a nursery school should compensate by spending large amounts of available time with the children. Extended periods of reading to them, weekends doing things together at home, and much listening and talking are musts. If weary parents avoid their children when they *are* together, the child is cut off from essential love and starves for the nurturing attention necessary for normal development.

Preparing the Child for School

The failproof concept mandates that the learner be motivated and prepared through progressive experiences so that he will be ready for each new undertaking. If failure is experienced, either motivation has not been accomplished or the task, based upon previous achievements leading up to it, has been inappropriate. Never is this more readily visible than when the child enters kindergarten or first grade. Many children arrive eager to participate while others are fearful and withdrawn, some to the point of physical illness. Some can take care of their physical needs and know how to play with other children, while others are confused and helpless. The difference is in how the child has been prepared for school.

The preparation process begins early in life as parents instill positive attitudes concerning school. It is described as a happy place where boys and girls have fun playing together; the possibility of unhappy situations is not discussed. Nor is school looked upon as separation from family but just an additional, natural step added to life because the child is growing up. "What fun it will be to go to school for a while and then come home to Mom and Dad to talk about the exciting things which happened there."

The air of anticipation grows as the child is taken for the orientation sessions prior to kindergarten. If he or she will be walking to school, several practice walks—with Dad or Mom, at first, with older brother or sister, later—should be done in the preceding months to give confidence and add to the anticipation. No negative element is permitted to enter the thinking. If immunization is necessary prior to entering school, the shots are gotten routinely—not for school, but because they are due. No connection should be made between this painful experience and school.

If older children relate negative experiences, these are debunked gently and without defensiveness. Parents should talk about how school was fun for them. Mention of holiday parties and toys at school are helpful—anything that emphasizes fun and positive feelings, but never anything negative.

Skills necessary for success in school should be taught systematically. Toilet usage, shoe tying, and how to play with others are examples of skills which are essential. If several kindergarten-age children live in the same neighborhood, it would be well for them to prepare as a group. Having others to walk with the first few days makes the going easier. If there is any reluctance the first or any day, use just as much firmness but no more than is necessary to overcome it, and get out of the picture as soon as possible. If you take the child to school, put him or her in the teacher's care and leave immediately. "I'll see you in a little while; have fun; I love you." This is all that needs to be said. Let the teacher take it from there.

Get To Know the Teacher

Pesky, overprotective parents are a bane to teachers; interested, involved parents are a great help. Parents must walk the tightrope between these two extremes. Blind submission to the will of the teacher can place the child in jeopardy and so can open disagreement. The leaning should be toward support of the school, which means always giving the benefit of the doubt to the teacher and withholding judgment until all the facts are known. There is nothing to be gained by having children be in the midst of a parent-school conflict. Any problems which arise must be handled privately so that the students retain maximum confidence in the school.

It is reasonable and advisable to get to know the teacher and find out what is happening in the class. Children learn far more from the way the teacher lives than from anything he or she says. Parents should visit the classroom when it is in session to see first-hand what is going on. No interference should occur and no remarks should be made during the time of the visitation. Such observations will be welcomed by professional teachers.

A good teacher is well organized and obviously in control, the methods of which are positive ones so that the resulting relaxed emotional atmosphere is conducive to learning. Warm, approachable, optimistic and enthusiastic about children and teaching, the love and respect of the teacher is noticeably present. Expectations of her pupils are high, but help and positive reinforcement are constant.

Love should be underscored as an absolute prerequisite to competent teaching. A teacher cannot teach unless he or she loves the students. Anything less becomes an exercise in futility where behavior changes, which is what education really consists of, will be neutral —even negative. Any success in mere fact memorization will be offset by lack of growth in student self-image. Persons who cannot genuinely love and respect all children should not be in teaching.

It will be up to parents, therefore, to deal with anything short of these standards. Confronting the issue may involve a change of teachers within the school. It may require a meeting with the principal, the superintendent or his representative, or even the school board. As a last resort, it may require placing the child in another school. For the sake of the child, who matures but once, bad teaching must not be condoned.

Working with Your School

The same emphasis should be applied when working with the entire school staff as with the individual classroom teacher. A cooperative spirit, harmony, mutual respect and praise are the goals. The most will be accomplished when parents and school personnel are very pleased with one another and the feeling openly expressed, for a positive environment brings out the best in everybody concerned.

Both parties must reach out to achieve this ideal. Without sacrificing principles, minor misunderstandings must be resolved quickly in a spirit of compromise. The school must do what is best educationally and without equivocation (and do it in a gentle manner—never one which is haughty or overbearing). Parents must recognize the obligation of equal treatment for all and never make requests which violate this standard. Every major decision should be preceded by this question: Everything else aside, what is best for the children? An honest response will keep all concerned on the right path.

SUMMARY CHECK LIST

1. Support the school but know what your child is doing.
2. Choose where to live based upon the quality of schools.
3. Avoid very large or very small schools.
4. Support school leaders who are statesmen; recall those who use the schools for their own purposes.
5. Make the beginning of school as normal as possible; don't talk about it excessively.
6. Don't imply that going to school is optional.
7. Try to find someone for the child to accompany to school rather than going alone.
8. If a private school is used, know whether it is a quality school or one established for misfits.
9. Keep infants at home until kindergarten, if possible; use nursery schools only as a last resort.
10. Don't put students in school earlier than is recommended by educators.
11. Systematically prepare the child for school by making him/her self-sufficient and sociable.
12. Prepare children for success in school: build pleasant anticipation; don't be overprotective.
13. Know your child's teacher and what and how she is teaching.
14. Visit the school and your child's class.
15. Always do what is best for the child, not what is expedient or what salves anybody's ego.
16. Don't disagree with the teacher or another staff member in the presence of the child. Explore concerns or disagreements privately.

Chapter 12

HOME CHORES

One of the best, and most often overlooked, opportunities to help children prepare for success in life is the proper assignment of home chores. This should be done, not just for the purpose of relieving parents of work and completing necessary tasks, but in a way that makes the maximum contribution possible to young persons. The assignment of these same jobs in an improper way not only robs young people of an opportunity to grow but it can also build negative attitudes which carry over into other areas of life and cause even more problems. We make jokes about young women who get married and are not able to take care of a home; we also poke fun at the young married man who cannot make even the most minor repair. These may be sources of humor for the comedian but they can also be causes of serious domestic problems.

Two hypothetical cases may serve to illustrate what can happen when chores are assigned properly and improperly. Admittedly, these are extreme cases and rarely would the job be done so well or so badly. In the first situation, the parents tried to do everything for their children rather than letting the children learn anything for themselves. Mother and Father waited on the children, picked up after them and tried to free them from any concern for their own self-maintenance or for helping other family members. Mother did all of the chores inside the house and Father did all the chores ouside the house while the children played, watched television, talked on the telephone and pursued other time-filling activities. Physical labor and manual skills were treated as second-class jobs compared to intellectual endeavors such as school work. When these children went off to college, they were disdainful of tasks which were necessary in that communal environment, creating conflict with their classmates. When the dormitory was given up in favor of apartment living, they were not able to cook or clean properly and this made life miserable. They had little preparation for marriage and the fundamental sharing of tasks and obligations which are so essential to happiness, but perhaps worst of all was the feeling these

91

children had toward their parents. Unwittingly, the parents had given their children the "welfare syndrome" because they had done everything for them, robbing them of their feeling of self-reliance. Rather than a legacy of independence, which is so essential in order for individuals to manage their own lives, these parents had turned out cripples who were retarded in self-management.

In our second hypothetical situation, quite the reverse was true. The parents lovingly taught their children to do all of the things possible as they grew through the various stages of maturity. They let them get the feeling of contributing to the family by doing meaningful chores not only to sustain themselves but, also, to help other family members. The children learned to cook, sew, clean and perform other tasks which are necessary in the maintenance of a home. These parents recognized that it would be a mistake to do anything for their children which they could do for themselves because this would deny them an opportunity to grow toward independence. A love for work well done, whether it was physical labor or intellectual endeavors, rounded their lives and they were ready to cope with the changing environment when they went away to college. They could take care of themselves in a situation which required adjustment and flexibility, and the chores which go along with establishing a family were no threat or mystery because they had been experienced while growing up. These children appreciated the wisdom which their parents had shown, and they were forever grateful for an upbringing which truly prepared them for life.

Goals of Work Assignments

The way work is assigned and the choice of tasks given should have, as a basis, certain goals which contribute to the maximum development of the child. Unfortunately, this approach is rarely taken. Generally, parents assign jobs sporadically and without any preplanning. Worse than this would be to assign jobs as punishment or in anger or inconsistently. Work which has a connotation of punishment will not result in maximum learning, positive self-image or a love for those activities which, by the nature of life, occupy so much of our time.

To make a maximum, positive contribution to life, home chores should have as bases at least some of the following goals:

1. Accomplishment of the tasks should result in a feeling of personal achievement because something new has been learned or improved.

2. There should be a feeling of contribution to another person or to the family unit.

3. The feeling of family interdependence and teamwork should be enhanced.

4. Relative difficulty of the tasks should be in sequence so as to promote a feeling of constant growth.

5. Tasks should be assigned in such a way that there is no connotation of punishment.

6. Children should get the feeling that they are "paying their own way" in life to prevent a "welfare syndrome."

These goals are important as we involve children at all ages, but they become especially crucial during adolescence. During this period, children are feeling a natural need to pull away from their parents, but the involvement in meaningful home chores will maintain a connection during these years and minimize the feeling of alienation. Adolescence is a difficult emotional period where children suffer the irony of feeling the need for independence while, at the same time, wanting the security of firm family connections. The conscious use of work at home can fill both of these requirements.

Tasks Should Be Appropriate to Maturity

One area which should get conscientious attention is the maturity level which is necessary to perform certain duties. If children are required to perform tasks before their physical development properly equips them, they will experience frustration and learn to dislike work. On the other hand, if only menial tasks are assigned even when the young person has ability beyond what is required, there is little sense of accomplishment and work becomes drudgery. It is true that there will always be menial tasks which all of us have to do, but mixed with them should be challenges which bring a feeling of growth and accomplishment when they are mastered.

Using home chores to help children grow and mature can begin very early in their lives. Babies love to help Mother and Dad and older children—and they can, by doing a simple part of a larger task. While Mother is straightening up his room, the child can put a book back in its place. When Dad is washing the car, the child can help by rubbing with a cloth one small area, such as a bumper or a headlight. The important thing is to increase the involvement as he grows so that an ever-increasing amount is done by him. It is also important to call attention to that part of the task which is actually "owned" by the children. A very young one will point to the car's bumper, which he washed all by himself, and express the same feeling of accomplishment which an older person would from washing the entire car.

The opportunity for family members to talk while joint tasks are being performed is very important. Attitudes are being learned and copied during these informal sessions, perhaps more than in our formal conversations. The work becomes secondary as we share the thoughts and feelings which develop an outlook on life which will be reflected much later.

Parents must be sensitive to the most helpful progression as ever-increasing involvement occurs. It is all right to have a son or daughter help to get breakfast ready by setting the table. This is exciting for the young child (as soon as he can reach) but it ceases to be exciting if this is the only thing that he is allowed to do. Once the rudiments of table setting have been mastered, it is time to move on to a more complicated and difficult task. Indeed, after a while, Mother or Father may want to do the table setting while the child prepares one of the dishes, creating an interest which will eventually lead to his planning and preparing an entire meal. Parents and children must do the work together, but it should be borne in mind that the child is the one who is growing. As he progresses to doing the more interesting elements of the tasks, the parents may have to shift back to the mundane things. In this way, the group continues to work together, promoting a feeling of teamwork and camaraderie, but the parents must be sensitive to adjusting their contributions in light of the needs and progressive accomplishments of the children.

Out of selfishness or ignorance, some parents teach their children how to work, the goal being a point where they, the parents, no longer have to do any of it. This would be a mistake because it violates what we are trying to do in terms of family interdependence and solidarity. All family members must continue to work together; at the same time, the children will progressively take on more difficult parts of the tasks until, ultimately, parents and children become equals, or peers, as the work is done.

Assignments Should Be Switched Periodically

In keeping with the sentiments expressed in the foregoing section, it is well to periodically change the assignments of family members so that all get an opportunity to do all of the jobs which need to be completed. Some chores have much more value than others and would be considered prime jobs compared to others which are held in much lower esteem. More is accomplished in terms of our goals for home chores if all family members get an opportunity to do all of them. This will contribute to the rounding of individuals so that their education is complete, and it will prevent the feeling that some family members are more highly regarded because they do the more important jobs. This rotation system also prevents boredom such as is experienced by assembly-line workers when they do the same job all of the time. It is also important to let each person exercise creativity and resourcefulness when work is undertaken. Parents would be well advised not to be too specific in describing how a job must be done. It is much better to describe in detail the outcome which is to be achieved, and then permit the person doing the task to exercise some individuality as long as the desired results are attained.

Avoid Sex Connotations in Assignment of Tasks

There is a tendency in our culture to attach strong sexual bias to the tasks which we assign boys and girls. It is traditional to teach girls to cook, sew and keep house while the boys learn to take care of the lawn and repair automobiles. A much better development of the young person will occur if we overcome this kind of sex stereotyping and subscribe to the position that both boys and girls have an opportunity to learn all of these things.

The important thing which is happening is the image which the young person is getting of himself. In high school, boys and girls will continue stereotyping themselves, often unconsciously. This is why girls in high school are reluctant to follow some of the math and science courses and, instead, defer to boys. There is really no logical reason to it; it is just an outgrowth of cultural stereotyping which was started much earlier in life. The root of such attitudes, which in the most extreme cases causes girls to set their goals lower in comparison to boys, comes from programming which began at a very early age. Parents who buy their small son a toy doctor's kit and their young daughter a toy nurse's kit are actually causing these young persons to formulate self-images later reflected in career goals and lifetime achievements.

The negative impact of early sex stereotyping can be avoided in great measure by letting children know there is no sex distinction inherent in any kind of work. Boys take their turns at cooking and cleaning and girls take their turns at using hand tools to make repairs and build things. Boys should be expected to make their beds and clean the bathroom on an equal basis with the girls. Girls should be taught to maintain and operate an automobile at the same ages and in the same way as boys. Parents should take every opportunity to make it abundantly clear that they support the idea of complete sexual equality. This involves being sensitive to even the most minor nuance of behavior. For example, if in our conversations we raise the question as to whether a girl will be able to combine marriage and a career, then the same question should be raised with regard to boys. During mealtime and other informal sessions, children of both sexes should take part in discussions of current events, world affairs, politics and finance on an equal basis. Interest in these subjects must first be generated at home so that continued curiosity can be established and both boys and girls will be knowledgable of them. If girls are encouraged to leave the table at these times, or if their opinions and questions are ignored or belittled, they will feel either that they must be irresponsible or else lacking in the skills necessary to discuss such relatively complicated topics.

Similarly, boys must not be excluded in the discussion of such topics as nutrition, child care, personal hygiene, or consumer buying. Whatever their principal role in the future, as responsible adults they will be required to understand healthful diets, the needs of children, prevention of disease and wise shopping habits.

As in all things which teach attitudes to children, the example set by the parents will be crucial. Children will always learn much more from what they see than from what they are ever told. In addition to the toys which we select for their early play, the chores which we assign and the topics which we discuss at mealtime, Mother and Father must also demonstrate in their daily lives that work is not sex-linked. If Father is the primary wage earner and Mother is the primary housekeeper, it must be made very clear to children that this was a conscious choice which grew out of their own values. Then as home chores are undertaken, they should be varied just as they are among children. Father must demonstrate by showing his skill at some of those things which are thought of as women's jobs and Mother must demonstrate her proficiency in what is, traditionally, man's work.

It is probably unrealistic for a man and woman who have been living traditional sex roles to make this kind of change quickly. Such a sudden change would not work because the two have not been prepared for the work involved, and it would probably not lead to the success which is important when it comes to teaching young people attitudes. For those who have not lived this way in the past, it would be better for the two to take an intense interest in what the other has been doing and show a willingness to learn and grow step-by-step, no matter what their ages. A beginning point has to come somewhere, and the children will realize that the two are consciously trying to master new skills. This in itself will reveal an attitude which will help the young persons make greater strides as they move toward the ultimate goal of having no sex stereotyping connected with tasks which are performed in our world.

Periodic Review and Reassessment

It is important for the family to sit down as a unit, periodically, and review what has been done and how things are going. This provides an opportunity to call attention to individual accomplishments; it is a systematic way of making sure that good work is not overlooked. It should be a positive session with the accent on achievement. Care must be taken to keep it from becoming a gripe session, but if any complaints do arise, they should be compassionately considered by the parents and adjustments should be made if workloads have been imbalanced.

The periodic review session is also the proper time for switching tasks and setting new goals. This should be a free-flowing session where the person who has had the task previously will give his replacement progress reports and hints for how the job can be done. Consideration should be given to individual preferences in the assignment of new tasks, wherever possible. As long as all family members get a chance to learn all of the jobs in the long range, it is most helpful if consensus is reached among the children as to the fairness of the work assigned; or better yet, let them do the assigning among themselves.

Participation of the children in the assignment of tasks has a very positive psychological affect. This story may illustrate the point: A brother and sister had difficulty dividing things fairly between each other. If a piece of cake was to be divided, one was always complaining that the other got the larger piece. If both shared the soft drink from one bottle, there was a complaint that more was poured into one glass than the other. This problem was solved forever when a very simple technique was employed: one youngster got the task of dividing the cake, and the other got first choice of selecting which piece he wanted. This assurance of fairness is a motivating factor, and it virtually eliminates the complaint that one person has been assigned more work than the other. Wise parents will define the work to be done and let the children agree on the assignments with the understanding that these will be traded periodically.

Excitement with Special Projects

Whenever a large or new task is to be undertaken, such as periodically painting the house, excitement and high motivation can be injected into the situation through the use of proper planning techniques. It is well to sit down as a group and look at the special project which is to be undertaken. Parents should not have preconceived ideas of the exactness of how the job is going to be done. Leaving as much detail as possible to selection by the entire group, the planning, deciding and preparing for the task creates excitement if all are allowed to participate. The children will hardly be able to wait to see their own ideas come to fruition as the job is done. What could be assigned drudgery if the parents did all the planning becomes a stimulating, corporate endeavor. Just as good school teachers use teacher-pupil planning as the first step in teaching, parents should do the same as they motivate the children toward their best efforts.

Patience, Flexibility and Compassion

The most successful parents will understand the fact that children are learners, and during the learning phase many mistakes are made. Since this is normal, children must be able to exist in an environment where they can make mistakes without being severely criticized or held in lower esteem. The way parents react to their children's mistakes often makes the difference in whether or not children will try again—and *trying is essential to growing*. So, the best approach for maximum growth is to accept mistakes as the natural order of things, compassionately help the youngsters overcome their mistakes, and be ready to let them try again with no reservation or undue attention to the errors.

SUMMARY CHECK LIST

1. Look upon assigned tasks as growth opportunities for children rather than just ways to get things done.
2. Make sure the jobs assigned are appropriate to the maturity level of the children.
3. Make sure the jobs are real, not just contrived, so that the children know that they are making a true contribution.
4. Switch assignments periodically so that maximum learning occurs in preventing one child from feeling that he has tasks of lesser value.
5. Avoid any sex stereotyping in the assignment of work. Let both sexes perform all tasks.
6. Have periodic reassessment meetings of the entire family to discuss progress and reassign work.
7. Praise all work done well and ignore mistakes as much as possible.
8. Participate in the doing rather than managing and evaluating.
9. Never assign work as punishment.
10. Make work schedules flexible with regard to school and church obligations.
11. Find something to praise, at least once a week.

Chapter 13

COMMON-SENSE RELIGIOUS TRAINING

It is a universal desire of human beings to attain immortality. In the ancient civilizations, even during humankind's early development, there existed the strong internal urge to rise above finite bounds. Similar to other basic drives, it is to some scholars yet another proof that immortality is possible, the idea being that no other drives are without a reason for existing, so why would the fundamental urge for immortality be the only pointless one?

Modern man pursues this impelling force in more sophisticated ways, but the basic concept is the same: Religious practice stems from the premise that there is a soul which survives the mortal body. Parents feel an obligation to teach children so they will have the tools—the faith—to also escape the punishment which results when salvation is not achieved, although, while they possess the urge, they do an abysmal job of achieving their goals, mainly, because of their own conflicting feelings and confusion.

Most are cautious enough to practice a little religion in case what they have been taught is true, but they are not sufficiently convinced to have religion make a real difference in their lives. Lip service to something with the potential impact of religion creates real dangers for children, so parents cannot afford to treat such an issue so lightly. The major cause of guilt in an individual is his own perception of violations of religious codes. The reduction of a person's potential for success is due to what he thinks is his failure to live up to religious standards enunciated by his parents when he was very young.

Religion As Behavior Control

A serious mistake made by many parents is to use religion for behavior control. It is true that religious concepts which are accepted by young people may affect behavior, but to use religious scare tactics results only in short-term control. The fear that "the boogieman will get you" might prevent certain behaviors for a while, but when reason overcomes this simplistic control, the fear and guilt will remain, at least subconsciously. It is far better for parents to handle behavior control themselves while children are young and let the effect of religious concepts influence his behavior after a child has matured enough to draw these connections independently.

This is not to say that a disciplined approach to religious practice and observance is bad—on the contrary. If religion is to be a part of the family's lifestyle, continuous performance of the rituals and constant participation are important.

Teach No More Religion
Than You Can Live

Worry, fear and similar emotions are threats to the failproof concept. Anything which preoccupies the mind unnecessarily makes it harder to maintain concentration and more difficult to become motivated to achieve maximum performance. Such emotions most often occur when the child feels he or she is not obeying the religious rules. They also occur when children see their parents violate rules which they have vowed to obey. If what parents say *should* be done is not what they do in reality, the child will worry about what might happen to them. If religious violators burn in Hell, a child is understandably concerned for the fate of parents who are obvious violators. To prevent this trauma, parents should neither teach nor permit to be taught more than they are willing to live. Religion preached strongly but practiced lightly is harmful. Parents who are not going to make their example a dedicated one should not bother teaching religion. The sermons children see are more important, and far more lasting, than the sermons they hear.

Logical Progression of Religious Concepts

The teaching of religion is no different from other training in that it should be systematic, continual and in progressive steps dependent upon the learner's maturity. The failproof approach to religion demands that no idea or concept precede the ability of the learner to handle that concept; moreover, motivation must accompany the training. This means, of course, that teaching the topic to little ones will need to be kept simple. When a child first asks, "What is God?" he should be answered plainly. "He is our Heavenly Father" or "He is a spirit we worship" will be enough for the time being. To go into a detailed discussion of the Trinity of God is beyond the needs or understanding of little ones.

Parents must also be careful to recognize when deeper explanations are necessary. Then the information should be given to the extent parents are able. It is imperative that parents not bluff about information they do not have or about beliefs they cannot explain logically. It is better to say "I don't know." Many religious practices are acts of faith copied from parents or religious leaders through tradition. It should not be an embarrassment to admit this. Children can deal with this better than untruths which, sooner or later, will become evident.

There are a number of fine books available for parents to use in telling stories of their faith to their children. Beautifully illustrated and simply worded, they are capable of leaving deep impressions upon young minds. These, supplemented by ritualistic observances will serve to indoctrinate a child. The inevitable questions can then be answered as he absorbs his newly found knowledge and begins to ponder upon it as he gains in maturity. In selecting stories, stay away from ones which contain violence or gory descriptions. Christ's death upon the cross, vividly described in bloody detail, is a horror scene which can scare and scar. Moreover, dealing with the wrath of God as it is described in the Old Testament is beyond the understanding of small children. The depiction of murder and treachery in the Bible will cause emotional trauma and create lasting damage in the immature mind.

For the same reason, young children should not be taken to funerals. Death is a most difficult reality even for adults. Children, not fully comprehending such an event, should be permitted to remember relatives and friends as they were when alive. As they gain in understanding, little ones will be better able to cope with the human emotions which are prevalent at burial services. Leaving them in the care of an understanding, sympathetic friend, who has been briefed about how to answer their questions, will be less injurious to them.

Unity in Family Faith Is Essential

Consistency, stability and predictability in everything concerning the home provide a security which contributes to the maximum growth of children, whereas conflict tends to produce insecurity which minimizes growth. Parents attending separate churches is a decidedly negative element when the atmosphere of security is considered. This is also the case if only one practices the custom. Any division between parents is detrimental, but when it involves a subject as emotional as religion, the potential harm becomes exacerbated. If one of the adults is an active participant, both should be. If one parent attends church, both should—and it should be the same church. For their children's welfare, responsible adults need to have this decision made and commitments given before children are brought into the world.

Know What Church School Teachers Are Teaching

Potential danger exists any time an immature mind is exposed to someone attempting to teach anything. Parents should have some knowledge of the people who are teaching their children, especially in a church-school situation where a lack of supervision and control may exist. In churches where there is little or no teacher training, many teachers are ill prepared to deal with young people. Some have little knowledge of what they are teaching or how to teach it.

Case in point: One family sent their child to Sunday School class each week while the adults attended the worship service. In their home, events in religious history were not given a literal interpretation as they would be in a fundamentalist doctrine. In addition, the family was liberal in regard to race relations—prejudice was avoided. In contrast, the Sunday school teacher was not only a fundamentalist, or literalist, but also a racial bigot. The child became confused and alarmed by this obvious conflict of teaching between home and church, so the experience led to deeper negative feelings about church school in general.

Some teachers morbidly take great pleasure in recounting the horror stories of the Old Testament, even to little children. The picture of Saul decapitated and impaled upon a fence is not appropriate for elementary-age children. Neither is a perfunctory attitude toward major concepts helpful. Denominational doctrine should be clearly enunciated in workshops and in materials used by teachers, who will then have the obligation to thoroughly instruct the learners. In the meantime, parents have the right to monitor the experiences of their children in all church activities.

Children and Worship Services

It is the custom in most religious denominations that corporate worship in a church sanctuary be conducted in a reverent, worshipful manner. It is unfair, though, to expect active, intelligent children to adhere to the standards of self-control practiced by older worshipers, particularly if learning to act in this manner is only required once a week between the time the clergyman first stands up and when he goes out the door. In the time span of a preschooler, the key word is *long*—a long time to have to sit on a hard pew without moving a muscle.

When the behavior of a squirming, fidgeting four-year-old becomes distracting enough to interrupt or embarrass parents, they may attempt to enforce unrealistic standards upon him, causing him to develop negative feelings toward church. Instead of quietly taking him out of the room at some appropriate point in the service, some parents, when their child's attention span runs out, proceed to "battle" with him until the service is over. He learns to associate going to church with the painful experience that results from tension and conflict between himself and his parents. Such a situation contributes nothing positive to anyone concerned, including other worshipers who are distracted by this type of behavior and, yet, are expected to tolerate it.

If anticipation and pleasure are to be associated with church, then parents must gradually introduce their children to it. Separate, brief worship as a part of the church school is one way to do this, or children can be taken to adult worship and then be excused, prior to the sermon, to go to another area for play, for a choral session, or for some other type of activity. This latter approach is probably a better one because it permits the family to be together for a portion of the worship service. A short exposure where young children can participate, but where they can leave before problems arise, is the most reasonable solution for all concerned.

Jesus, Santa Claus and the Tooth Fairy

It is not intended that the title of this section connect the Deity with a Christmas legend nor be sacrilegious.

It *is* intended to point out just one problem than can be incurred by parents as they attempt to rear children in a religious mode among the modern trappings which are a part of our secular world. An attempt is also made to demonstrate that the failproof concept must be stringently adhered to if it is to succeed.

Small children, trusting by nature, are easily duped by adults who take advantage of their gullibility. Moreover, they are never more vulnerable than when parents tell them untruths.

Following tradition, parents tell their children how Santa Claus brings the presents at Christmas. They use him as a threat to make them behave— "Everyone KNOWS only GOOD little children get presents." There are even people who threaten their children with "Santa's not bringing you anything but sticks and stones, you bad boy!"—at the slightest infraction of household rules. Parents also tell their youngsters how the tooth fairy rewards them for teeth which fall out (or have to be extracted). Both of these spirits, and others like the Easter Bunny, are unseen; belief in them requires faith.

During this same impressionable period of life, religion is being taught. Children learn that Jesus or God are good spiritual beings who help them while demanding certain behavior of them in order to remain in good graces. With faith and trust they believe this, even though there is no proof Jesus or God can be seen or heard.

There will come a time when the Santa Claus myth is exposed, revealing the truth. Children will reject the reality at first; this is a shock which is not easily overcome, but, sooner or later, the horrible truth is accepted: there is no Santa Claus.

A child then may begin to reason by wondering what other lies he has been told. "When are they going to tell me the other spirits are only fakes?" he will ask himself. "How can I ever believe adults again?"

Children are very logical in their thinking, and they are free of subtleties and ambiguities. It is natural that doubt about any unseen spirits will be the outcome of the Santa Claus deception. Can parents justify this lie in any plausible way? Of course not. Faith in parents, which is so essential to a positive relationship, has been violated. It will never be the same again.

How can this be avoided? How can trust in parents — a trust so vital to the security which goes with failproofing — be preserved? It is really quite simple. The lie about Santa Claus need never be told in the first place. Just as much fun could be had if parents had said from the beginning, "We are Santa Claus. It's just a game we play at Christmas. We dress up and give you presents and tell these 'pretend stories' about chimneys and reindeer to add to the fun."

There would be no loss in excitement about Christmas and about presents, but the big lie would be avoided. More important, there would not be a basic distrust of other things not seen such as the spiritual beings of religious worship. The fact that Christmas and the Santa Claus visit are simultaneous makes it even more important for Christmas not to employ the Santa Claus myth. The chance for carry-over of the myth into the religious tenets is too great.

SUMMARY CHECK LIST

1. Don't use religion to control children's behavior.

2. Teach no more religion than you are willing to live.

3. Prevent religious guilt feelings in the young.

4. Protect children from religious horror stories.

5. Teach religious concepts progressively.

6. Don't attend separate churches; it confuses the child.

7. Don't take little children to funerals.

8. Know what church school teachers are teaching.

9. Introduce children to worship services gradually, based upon their attention spans.

10. Require children to behave when they are in church.

11. Don't represent Santa Claus as a fact; make it a game from the start.

Chapter 14

SPORTS COMPETITION

The scene is a sports-club game in a city somewhere in the United States on a Saturday morning. Hundreds of screaming parents are watching their nine-year-olds playing baseball. The children are arrayed in splendid uniforms and are using the latest and most expensive baseball gloves and bats. Coaches parade on the sidelines loudly exhorting and harshly criticizing the children as they attempt to perform to please parents and coaches alike. Umpires, as they try to enforce the rules of the game, are subjected to the vehement oral attacks of spectators.

Shouts of "Throw one close to his head!" "Go in with spikes flying!" and "The umpire is a crook!" emanate from the benches. A boy strikes out and walks back to the dugout—head down and tears in his eyes—because he has failed. The game ends with one team embraced by proud and happy parents; the other team walks in silence except for the recriminations of parents who vow revenge "one way or another." An exaggeration? Not to anyone who has witnessed this American tragedy.

The devastating effect of such an experience is not much different from that of a small girl whose mother yells at her for "losing" a beauty contest. Nor is it different from the parent who screams at a child for not learning to ride a bike "fast enough."

In organized sports, the increased pressure which occurs in group participation creates an additional dimension of trauma for children, so that as a result of the widespread availability of team sports, there arises a potential danger for large numbers of children, particularly in highly populated areas.

Readiness for Team Sports

Placing young children in team competition in football, baseball, or similar sports is a violation of the failproof concept because it gives them tasks beyond their level of readiness. The muscles required to perform the complicated movements have not matured sufficiently. Instead of a baseball—which is quite small—a large softball, which is easier to grasp, would be more appropriate for small children to use. When tasks are given which go beyond the ability of children to do well, either poor performance or total failure is likely to result, causing psychological harm—the greatest danger of all. If mental pressure placed upon children by their parents is also present, there results a situation which is indefensible.

Young children need physical activity but it must match their maturation level, physically and emotionally. This means providing coeducational games involving the use of large muscles so that the emphasis can be placed upon coordination and sense of rhythm. Using large balls for throwing, for catching and kicking, and running in short spurts, such as in relay games, are also helpful to their growth. While these activities may not do much for adult ego-satisfaction, they are what the children need.

Competition with oneself is helpful during these years as long as unwholesome pressure is not applied. Children should try to swim faster, jump farther or achieve higher scores in gymnastics. If parents will monitor these activities, they can help their children set reachable goals in a progressive fashion rather than setting them beyond the point of frustration. Without using time limits, children can set for themselves a few seconds less, another foot, or one step of a more difficult technique. When that goal is reached, another can be set. By moving one step at a time, the effects of self-confidence will result in nothing less than the reward of success.

Danger of Permanent Injury

Contact sports are particularly hazardous for children at the age of adolescence and below. Studies of the developing human body reveal that bone ends are still soft, that an injury which might readily heal in later life will become a permanent deformity if experienced during this period. If contact sports are not to be avoided, then superabundant care must be given to preliminary conditioning and to protective equipment. The toy helmets and shoulder pads which are worn by some small boys in tackle football offer no real protection. Worse yet, they give a false feeling of security which causes the participants to be more reckless than they would be with no equipment at all.

Proper Goals for Competition

Competition has an important role in the growth of the young. Nothing discussed here is meant to imply that proper competition which is adjusted to the maturity level of the learner is bad. Particularly in the free enterprise system of the United States, competition contributes to learning a winning lifestyle. Competing must be instinctive if young people are to survive, secure a job, earn money or be admitted to college. The challenge becomes that of teaching children skills of competition without harming them by using the wrong activities or by starting too early.

110

Competition should help children extend themselves to reach a goal. It should teach them to desire success, to be assertive instead of acquiescent and, at the same time, to play according to established rules. Winning loses its value if rules are ignored or if cheating is employed. Learning to win unfairly means trouble ahead because in the adult world, such behavior generally leads for punishment or, at least, to social ostracism. The coach who teaches "win at any cost" either by precept or example is not teaching proper competition and is actually doing the learner a terrible disservice.

The example at the beginning of the chapter illustrated unwholesome competition where negative attitudes were being taught. Why would adults do this to innocent children? There is no one answer, but the most prevalent cause is adult ego-satisfaction. Either the parents or the coach, or both, have placed *winning* the game above every other aspect. If these adults would only stop to realize that the winning is not nearly as important as the attitudes being learned, they could quickly put the situation into proper perspective. The score of the game may not long be remembered, but the children will be playing the game of life according to the attitudes they learn in the games. Parents must get their own egos under control, and they must be very careful of the coaches who work with their children. The process is the important element. Children are learning patterns for living. They must not be secondary to winning.

Programs of Sports Competition

Sports activities are an important part of an adequate school program. They contribute to good physical health and to emotional adjustment. Unfortunately, many school programs are built around competition between schools and thus do not have value for the masses of young people. Even physical education classes in some schools are used as training grounds for athletes. This limits the program to major team sports. It overlooks the needs of a majority of students who are not a part of school teams.

Wholesome competition has value for all students, not just the physically elite. Interscholastic competition, which involves such a small percentage of the total school population, is not designed to meet the needs of the majority of students. In addition, the fact that schools are much larger than in the past limits the chance to compete to only a few outstanding athletes. This means the ones who need it least are the ones who are being served. So, what is really needed is a system of intra-school competition for all ability levels—in a variety of sports. In this way, the masses can be served appropriately in accordance with their needs.

This is not a proposal that varsity athletics be eliminated, or even curbed. It is a proposal that schools stop letting the "tail way the dog" by putting major emphasis on interschool competition. Varsity sports should be the accelerated activity for the physically gifted. Just as only a few students pursue advanced mathematics, only a few pursue accelerated sports. To have no program of sports competition for average students is like having no math classes except for the exceptionally gifted!

Some schools do spend money, allocate staff and publicize intramural sports designed to serve all students regardless of ability. Unfortunately, this is the exception rather than the rule. Parents must use whatever means is necessary to change the present system which ignores most students. Even gifted athletes are harmed by a system which exploits them to satisfy the egomania of coaches.

In particular, attention should be given to middle and junior high schools because this is where the majority of students lose interest in sports competition. Here is where it is imperative that "no-cut" rules be enforced, thus assuring that all who have an earnest desire to participate in school teams will not have to try out for them. Middle school is far too soon to expose children to the emotion of being "cut" from a team.

Physical Education Instruction

Athletics and physical education instruction should be two distinctly different subjects because physical education is so much more than taking part in sports. Good physical education classes use physical activities to teach everything from healthful living to cooperation and democracy. Sports programs should be kept separate so the instructional phase remains pure.

Elementary physical education helps children master muscle movement as they participate in games. Progressively difficult physical responses are required as the children grow, and competition and cooperation are emphasized but with *fun* always a goal. When physical activity ceases to be fun, the activity tends to be avoided—which creates an undesirable effect because the human body demands periodic vigorous physical activity for maximum health.

As children grow and desire greater competition, intramurals should be available for all of them; athletic teams should be provided in high school for those who excel. The emphasis in physical education classes would differ each year rather than each year being a repetition of the previous one. When formal schooling draws to a close in the latter years of high school, much attention should be given to the teaching of carry-over sports which will be pursued for a lifetime. Tennis, swimming, jogging, golf, handball, table tennis, bicycling and similar sports are taught because most of these can be followed without extensive cost, equipment or other persons. The major sports have very little value in terms of carry-over into later life. Here again, as in all of this discussion dealing with sports, of the most significance will be the process and the attitudes which persist after the activity ceases. Not only will this determine whether the activity is repeated, but the whole self-image which results will spill over into all of life.

SUMMARY CHECK LIST

1. Try to prevent small children from participating in team sports.
2. Emphasize physical activity which uses large muscles, disperses excess energy and results in fun.
3. Teach games which involve competition with self.
4. If children do play contact sports, make sure equipment is of the highest quality and appropriate to the child's size.
5. Always remember that the process is more important than the game scores because the attitudes carry over into all of life.
6. Demand that proper emphasis be given to intramurals in school.
7. Do not permit athletic programs to use a disproportionate amount of school funds.
8. Require wholesome physical education instruction in all grades of school.
9. Install "no-cut" policies in middle or junior high school team-sport programs.
10. Emphasize lifetime sports in the senior high physical education curriculum.

Chapter 15

GIFTED CHILDREN

Parents who discover that they have a gifted child are often elated by the prospects for the future. Unfortunately, the elation turns to sadness in many cases. Intellectual potential is not a destination; it is the beginning of what can be a treacherous journey. As with anything affecting children, the differences between happiness and success or heartbreak and failure are the actions taken by parents and other adults. "Fertile soil grows weeds as readily as flowers." Giftedness is a special challenge which must be constantly examined and managed with great care.

Anything which makes a person different can become a plus or minus factor: physical handicaps, in some instances, actually increase motivation; an unusual name can be made a trademark rather than a cause for derision. A special characteristic can either become positive or negative, depending upon whether it is used to advantage or accepted passively. Giftedness is an unusual condition so it falls into the category of "specialness." It may even be compared to a handicap in that it requires adjustments in behavior.

What Is Giftedness?

Definitions of giftedness vary, but in most cases the reference is to generally possessing a high degree of intellect, and it is usually expressed in terms of an intelligence quotient (the ratio of tested mental age to chronological age), thus measuring intellectual ability only. An I.Q. of 100 is considered average; 120, above average; 140, gifted. Since these are broad categories, opinions vary as to where the lines of demarcation fall, but the differences in definition are not nearly the problem as the tests themselves. To begin with, most results are approximations even when the tests are properly administered. It will suffice to say that an individual's score could be well above or below the assigned number for a variety of reasons.

A better way to describe giftedness is in behaviorial terms. Bright children are quick in mastering abstract concepts. They may read spontaneously from exposure to books without previous formal instruction; they will verbalize readily and remember facts with relative ease. Average children who receive a great deal of attention as infants and who are exposed to highly verbal parents may show these signs, but purely precocious behavior tends to plateau at an early age; the truly gifted continue to master abstractions throughout their lives. This fact should be a warning to parents not to jump to conclusions based only upon early outgoing behavior.

The image of a mentally acute individual generally includes "labels" such as "egghead" or "bookworm." These are stereotypes and have no basis in fact. Children can be bright and be outgoing or timid, depending upon how they have been taught to behave. The fact that many bright children are termed "eggheads" says something about our success in dealing with them. It is a negative image resulting from our failures.

What Are the Needs of Gifted Students?

Gifted students' needs vary little from those of all young people: peer acceptance, a comfortable feeling about themselves, love, praise and a feeling of complete normalcy. A high degree of intelligence assures none of these; it can even make their accomplishment more difficult.

The child with a keen mind will always find intellectual challenges easier to conquer than will students of average ability. While study should not be discouraged, the other needs which are being felt are also essential for normal development.

This means that parents will need to give greater attention to these other needs which will not be met spontaneously as will things intellectual. It is a tragic mistake to emphasize an area which needs the least attention while others go unattended. Not only does it contribute to the negative stereotyping of the bright student as a "bookworm," but the bright child who is crippled by a lack of normal survival skills cannot be a productive adult.

No attempt is made to list all of the skills crucial to success, but several are given as examples:

1. Social Skills
All children need to learn to get along in this social world. The bright child needs to be given the opportunity to work and play with those less intelligent. Communication is an important tool but it takes practice, so he must be encouraged to participate in a variety of activities which are enjoyed by all children. Isolation will diminish these essential social skills, producing a retiring, timid adult.

2. *Physical Skills*

Some parents are opposed to having their talented children participate in sports because it takes time away from more cerebral pursuits. This is a mistake; physical skill development is natural and as much a need for the bright child as for any other. A good way to be a part of the youth culture is to be skilled enough to participate in physical activities. The bright child who excels as a swimmer, or a tennis or football player is more readily accepted by his less intellectual peers.

3. *Self-reliance Skills*

The assurity of self-confidence is crucial to success. In academic endeavors, a knowledgeable person will have an acute sense of self-confidence, but this is not enough; he must be able to become an active participant in many activities. From public speaking to caring for a lawn—whatever the area may be—the important thing is to know he can hold his own in all of life.

Parent Egos Can Be Dangerous

Parents must realize that the welfare of their highly intelligent children demands that parental egos be kept in check. There is a natural tendency to boast about the good fortune of having a bright child, but this is repugnant to most people and merely creates resentment. To make matters worse, if this attitude is imitated by the child himself, it creates peer problems for him.

The many uncontrollable variables which result in the birth of a gifted child rule out any reason for bragging. These same variables could have created a slow learner, perhaps a mentally retarded child. The parents' attitude should be one of quiet gratitude and modesty rather than braggadocio. Possessing an air of arrogance would be taking credit for God's work.

Parents of gifted children are often demanding of schools and of others with whom their children come in contact. "My child is very bright, you know, so he will just have to have a teacher who can challenge him" is often expressed, either nonverbally or in not-so-subtle terms. Since there is no logical reason for this kind of demand, the reaction can be only negative; no one appreciates, nor will he be able to tolerate, such a posture. Much more will be accomplished when parents are cooperative. Schools must provide good programs for all children, no matter what their needs. The whole system cannot be bent to the requirements of a single group, whether it be bright, average, or of low ability. Those needs will be best served if parental egos are controlled so that rational consideration can be given to providing for all children equally.

117

School Programs for the Gifted

This topic can be best presented by this writer's earlier article on the subject:

In Texas, a very bright junior high student brings a rifle to school and kills his English teacher with three well-placed shots; the reason: The teacher had mildly criticized him earlier in the week. An Iowa student graduates at the top of her class and ends up in an asylum less than a year later because she cannot take the increased competition in college. A boy in Maryland commits suicide rather than accept a grade lower than he thinks he should have received. All of these young people were rapid learners who were crippled by well-intentioned programs designed for very intelligent children—programs which denied them exposure to the real world and a chance to learn to cope with the adversities which confront us during the normal course of life.

Leadership positions in business, government and the professions—positions which should be filled by our brightest citizens—are occupied, instead, by people of average or little-more-than-average intelligence. The correlation between superior intellect and insanity appears higher than the one between intelligence and success. These inconsistencies between ability and achievement probably stem from a variety of causes, but we in professional education must assume our share of the blame. In truth, our programs for rapid learners are producing disastrous results—most students would be better off never having been exposed to them.

What is wrong with the programs?

Take a look at the accelerated program in your local school. Chances are that it is narrow, centering almost entirely upon increasing intelligence. Physical and social skills are ignored, so the child becomes physically retarded and a social misfit. To make matters worse, other students may chide him, turning him into a withdrawn, morose individual.

Ignoring the area of need and sheltering the students from the real world of average people results in the reduced ability to cope with life's challenges. This is comparable in approach to denying a handicapped child any opportunity to develop unaffected body parts to compensate for the handicap. Following this theory with a blind child, for example, we would never consider restoring balance and a semblance of normalcy by stressing greater than average development of the senses of touch and hearing.

The value of brightness is lost unless a child can compete with other children in all areas of endeavor. He needs a balance of physical and emotional development; he does not need programs which make him different, which prompt others to refer to him as an "egghead."

Why have these programs evolved?

Pressure from parents upon school administrators and boards of trustees is the main reason why this situation has been allowed to develop. The parents are eager to serve their own ego needs, and it is always more pleasant to say yes than no to their requests. It is parental ego that wants kids in school at age four or five, wants them coddled and protected. Most parents mean well, but they are ignorant of the long-term detrimental effects of such things upon their children.

Current school programs create an attitude among the participants to believe that life will always be on their terms, to expect special treatment which has not been earned, and to assume they will have freedom from rules and regulations. Such an attitude can, of course, lead to disaster for the young person.

Educators know better; they must have the courage to do what they know will be best for the students. They are very much aware that these same parents are spoiling their bright children by not requiring that they perform "mundane" chores around the house—that they are treating them as guests in their own home. The result will be tragic. Becoming adults, they will expect the "world on a platter," but, of course, this is not the way they will find it. Our society is built upon competition, upon rewards in keeping with our contributions. Children, bright or not, cannot grow up expecting to be on the receiving end without earning their way.

What would be a good program for bright children?

Intelligent boys and girls should not be denied intellectual growth in the arts or sciences. Their talents will naturally lead them in that direction, but there are other areas which are just as important. All children need to be accepted by others their own age if they are to grow into well-adjusted adults. They must be "mainstreamed"— which is a term used for justifying placement of handicapped children in a school with normal children. They can, and should be, given enrichment activities but in the areas of need which are peculiar to bright children—in athletic activities, in manual skills. They must be given the opportunity to learn perseverance, a skill not normally acquired because learning comes so easily to them. They must also learn to cope by meeting and solving adversities; they must not be unduly sheltered. The world-at-large will not care how intelligent a person is; it will expect him to manage his own problems.

119

A group of very bright students was taken on an Outward Bound program where hard work, self-reliance and survival skills had to be learned or students were dropped. Those who completed this rugged course came to know themselves. They learned what it means to compete on "grit" and tenacity rather than brains alone. With their keen minds and the development of these kinds of skills and attitudes, those young people will not waste their gifts by becoming social outcasts or psychological cripples.

SUMMARY CHECK LIST

1. Treat giftedness as a challenge rather than an accomplishment.

2. Teach gifted students how to get along in a world where most people are average, where their success will depend upon how they are accepted by average people.

3. Place the emphasis upon becoming well rounded. Develop social and survival skills.

4. Provide bright students with more opportunities for learning perseverance and for mastering that skill.

5. Don't allow inflated egos; they create harmful attitudes.

6. Avoid school programs for the gifted which are based primarily upon parental demands rather than the true needs of learners.

Chapter 16

THE CHILD'S BILL OF RIGHTS

Parents may think of their parenting role as a service to children. There is no question that children's needs are best served when parents meet their obligations, but parenthood is a voluntary service with the children being the ones who have no choice. Parents are not obliged to produce children, but children cannot exercise a right not to be born. Therefore, a new outlook is needed upon the relative obligations of parents and children to each other.

This philosophy is the failproof theory. Based upon this premise, when children do not accomplish something, we look to adults who have assigned an inappropriate task rather than to the child who received it. It shifts the responsibility to the adults--where it should be. In this same vein, the parents must look to their obligations to children before they consider the children's obligations to them. This is the proper sequence; parents must do their job completely before the children can be held accountable for responding to parental expectations.

This means that children have rights—primary rights which come to them for no other reason than that they were born. Parents must respect these rights and make whatever sacrifices are necessary to see that they are fully realized. Success of the offspring requires this; anything less increases the possibility of failure. A bill of rights for children must be adopted by parents if failproofing is to succeed.

Unconditional Love

Every child requires the nurturing warmth of parental love. It must come with no strings attached and without regard to the level of intelligence, physical appearance, type of personality or handicapping condition of the child. Conditional love stunts wholesome growth and encourages psychological abnormalities. Behavior of the child need not always be accepted, but the person as an individual must be. This distinction must be clear; rejection of unacceptable behavior must not imply any rejection of the person.

The flow of parental love cannot be controlled as one might control the flow of water by turning a spigot. It is not an instrument of exchange to be given in return for something else. It is a basic right just as the right of citizenship is possessed, based only upon where we are born. No threat should ever be made suggesting that love might be lessened in a given set of circumstances. All children in a family must have a full measure and an exactly equal portion. Unless care is exercised in achieving this equality, a child who may seem difficult to love may get less when, in reality, his need for it is greater.

Interpretation of Self

The world is a mystifying place to a child. Every day brings new experiences which need to be codified and fed into that greatest of all computers—the human brain. This takes interpretation, and assistance is required to do it properly by making right judgments. The feelings within a child add to the puzzle called life and require additional adult guidance. "Who am I; where do I fit into the scheme of things?" are questions which must be resolved during the growth process.

Parents should begin by letting each child know he is a part of a world that is basically good, that people can be trusted and helpful in most situations. This gives him a positive outlook on life, reflected as in a mirror because the world tends to respond to *our* cues. There will be plenty of time to warn the child against the problems of the world as he or she grows in independence and responsibility.

Children also have a right to strong family membership--*strong* meaning a place of importance in the family. It makes little difference whether it is a large or small family or a one or two-part family; whatever the makeup of the unit, each child must feel as important as any other member. That will require sincere acceptance by all of the family members, without equivocation. It will require special efforts by family members if one child is handicapped in any way; he must interpret his situation as one of obvious belonging.

This leads to the person's interpretation of self. On the one hand, the perception must be that he or she is normal in terms of behavior but, at the same time, special for some reason. This requires a wholesome love of self—wholesome so as to avoid narcissism but sufficiently assured with himself to possess confidence. An inner feeling of contentment is essential in preventing diffidence so that the child can try something new. Love of others is not really possible unless wholesome self-love is present. Children must be taught this; self-respect must not be thought of as negative.

Protection from Trauma

Exposure to frightening childhood experiences can result in permanent psychological damage. Much of the therapy done by psychiatrists involves going back into childhood through psychoanalysis to uncover and remove the effects of some traumatic experience which is providing a negative influence years later. The immature mind must be protected from trauma; parents owe this to their youngsters—they are too young to exercise self-protection.

Some of the more common sources of childhood trauma are:

1. Adult Concerns

Parents who discuss economic difficulties or interpersonal conflicts in the presence of children can readily transmit their concern. It is then often blown out of proportion in the child's mind because the parent seems threatened, and the parent is the basic source of security to him.

2. Horror Stories

Fairy tales which tell of violence will capture the interest of children but can result in nightmares. There are numerous happy stories which can be told without risk of harmful side effects.

3. Television

Children can gain much from television if parents are selective in what the children are permitted to watch. Any program, whether cartoon or with live actors, should be avoided if it contains terror, violence or conflict. Parents should watch television with their children rather than let it be an electronic babysitter. Not only will this produce camaraderie but it makes possible desirable parental monitoring.

4. Funerals, Accidents, etc.

Such events are difficult to endure even for adults and, certainly, they are beyond the readiness of small children. Although they are a part of living and we must learn to deal with them realistically, trauma-creating events should not be imposed upon children.

Individuality

Each child needs to feel unique as an individual human being. This is particularly true if there are several children in a family. This means no comparisons should be made between children, and it means that each should be encouraged to develop skills which are unique.

There will be exceptional situations where several children excel at the same activity, and no attempt should be made to discourage this if it evolves naturally. But, generally, the younger child is at a disadvantage because of the age difference and level of accomplishment, so the comparison is negative. He or she does not realize that, when adjustment is made for the difference, he is actually doing well. Frustration is therefore less likely if children have diverse areas of major interest.

Parents must be careful not to value one specialty over another because of their own biases. Sports-minded Dad must be just as thrilled with the musical accomplishments of one child as he is with the sports achievements of another. The goal is to have both feel the complete acceptance and approval of their parents.

Teachers are often guilty of prejudging younger brothers and sisters of their former students. Rather than recognizing each child as an individual, they tend to lump them into one mold. It is risky to assume that one child is exactly like another merely because they come from the same family. A wise teacher will make only positive comparisons, if any.

Accomplishment

It is pointed out elsewhere that a feeling of personal accomplishment is essential to a happy and successful life. This is why parents must refrain from doing everything for their children and, instead, take extra time to teach them how to do things for themselves. Basic to a sense of accomplishment is ability, so this means skills must be taught, but parents will need to select skills appropriate to maturity levels and see that children are motivated and trained.

Young people often have intense interests in activities such as sports; parents can use these as starting points. New areas can also be explored if the adults are willing to take the lead. At least two important commitments are required of parents if they are to provide opportunities which bring a feeling of accomplishment:

1. Time
One sure indicator of how serious a person is about a given matter is the time he or she is willing to put into it. (Incidentally, children sense that time is spent on priority matters, so this is one important way they gauge parental love.) If children are to be adequately taught and have sufficient practice, under observation, parents must be willing to devote a sizable block of time on a regular basis. If one is unwilling to do the job right by giving enough time, it would be better not to raise hopes and create enthusiasm. Disappointment over a broken promise is worse than never having been promised in the first place.

The mother who is teaching a son or daughter to play chess should spend several periods each week for a year or more so the skill is mastered enough to bring pride in an accomplishment which exceeds that of others. The father who is teaching ping pong to his child must play with the youngster repeatedly and regularly for the same reason.

2. Patience

The great killer of teaching and of learning is *Impatience*. Many attempts at teaching by parents go sour when they do not have the patience to wait for mastery by the learner. The failproof theory teaches that if a skill is not mastered, the teacher has not chosen a task appropriate to either the previous experiences or level of motivation of the learner.

Freedom from Guilt

Agonizing guilt is a debilitating force. Talents go unused because withdrawal gives more protection; reticence overcomes natural assertiveness and time is spent worrying rather than creating. Guilt is a natural reaction for everyone at some time or other because of the world in which we live. Society imposes a myriad of rules, regulations and formal laws. Religion adds other beliefs and traditions, even more. Avoiding everything which causes guilt is impossible, yet it must be conquered for maximum success in living. Help must be given to children if they are to deal with guilt; these suggestions will aid in overcoming it:

1. Forgive yourself first.

Every human being—every creature—is worthy of forgiveness; this is taught by every major religion and philosophy. Does it not follow that a person must also forgive himself? Logic not only supports self-forgiveness but also implies that it is essential if we are to be effective forgivers of others. The ability to be reasonable in forgiving oneself is an important growth idea.

2. Making mistakes is normal.

It is human nature to assume that our own mistakes are, somehow, unique. It leads to an attitude of guarding our past indiscretions lest someone else discover our secrets. The truth is that mistakes are common to *all* people. Rather than looking for our failures, others are guarding their own errors. The comfort of knowing that all people share feelings of insecurity because of past actions releases us to venture and grow. Children need to understand this and to put their shortcomings into proper perspective.

3. Live each day.

Statistically speaking, much of what we fear never happens. Worries about the future are usually exaggerated: human ingenuity is equal to even the severest of challenges. This fact must be accepted so that today is not spent regretting past failures and worrying about the future. It sounds like an oversimplified idea but it is true: Living each day "to the hilt" is the best way to overcome yesterday's problems and avoid tomorrow's threats.

Health and Safety

The implication of the word *infant* is a person incapable of self-determination or self-protection. Human offspring are unique in the long amount of time they are incapable of caring for themselves. Parents, in their decision to become parents, assume responsibility for the constant care of offspring for a period of many years. Children are taught to care for themselves in gradual steps as they are capable, the goal being the achievement of self-reliance.

During the years of dependence, parents must conscientiously see to the health and safety of children; it is an inalienable birthright. It requires supervision to prevent accidents, diet control to maintain good health and the teaching of behavior and health practices which evolve into supportive habits and attitudes. Immunizations and dental exams must be taken care of as a matter of routine; it should not even be discussed that these necessities are in any way optional.

Special attention must be given to the types of games which children are permitted to play. Toys which are inherently dangerous, i.e., those which have sharp points, parts which can be swallowed or toxic-paint finishes are examples of potentially harmful items. Those which propel projectiles such as darts or arrows are not suitable playthings for little ones. It is too late to act after an eye is lost, so even such innocent looking implements as pencils and paintbrushes can be highly dangerous. Though the most conscientious supervision cannot prevent all accidents, the awesome task of trying is an obligation for all who assume parenthood.

Economic Support

The cost of rearing children continues to increase at an even greater rate than that of inflation, and a greater portion of family resources is being allocated to their needs. Economic planning will be necessary in order to meet these requirements.

First and foremost will be the need for prenatal care. Prospective parents of today realize how vital it is that a pregnancy's progress be constantly monitored by a physician, not only for the sake of the fetus but for the mother as well. Both have this right. It is important, too, that the father-to-be join in this process--both mother and father are embarking upon a long, dedicated career. After the baby is born, visits to the doctor must continue. Not only can the many questions from the new parents be answered, but good habits of nutrition and hygiene must be established. Important immunizations must begin. Wise parents are fighting the battle against dreadful childhood diseases with early inoculations for their children. Through the use of preventive medicine during the prenatal period and beyond, parents are producing healthier, happier, brighter citizens.

With preventive medicine, many necessities have emerged which were once considered luxuries. Orthodontia is now assumed to be necessary; a few years ago it was unusual to see a child with braces on his teeth. Continued medical care throughout childhood will need to be maintained. To provide the means for financing it will take careful planning.

Adequate schooling is another example. A minimal education once produced economic self-sufficiency, but this is no longer true. Fewer jobs for the unskilled have made more education a fundamental requirement. The increased costs of a post-high school education and the prolonged period of dependency mean that the family must pay current costs and, at the same time, save for the inevitably increased costs of the future.

Nothing is more fundamental than the right of children to be economically secure while growing up and then to have support while getting the education necessary for independence. This will require sacrifices by most families in order to meet these needs adequately. There is no choice in the matter; children should not live in luxury, but adequate financial support comes at the very top of family financial priorities.

A CHILD'S BILL OF RIGHTS

The basic rights provided by responsible parents for their children are:

1. Unconditional love

2. Interpretation of self

3. Protection from trauma

4. Individuality

5. Accomplishment

6. Freedom from guilt

7. Health and safety

8. Economic support

APPENDIX I

BUILDING POSITIVE ATTITUDES IN LEARNERS

A Series of Informal Conversations

with the Author

HOW CAN PARENTS
BUILD POSITIVE ATTITUDES?

Question:

Dr. Fitzwater, I would like to begin our conversation by discussing the proper home environment for the development of positive attitudes in children; but first, what is a positive attitude as it relates to learning? How can we tell when a young person has such an attitude?

Answer:

The youngster with a positive attitude shows confidence, has a feeling of adequacy, and goes into a new activity with an expectation of success. It is said that success builds success, and that is certainly true. The youngster with a positive attitude expects things to turn out right, and they generally do because of that expectation. The child with a positive attitude will approach a new subject in school and expect to succeed. It is amazing but very true—we can usually do anything we *think* we can do. Conversely, if we think we can't, we won't. The child with a positive attitude is optimistic, enthusiastic, and eager to try new things.

Question:

Well, do attitudes come totally from our environment, or is some of this inherited?

Answer:

Certainly, basic abilities with which we are born help us. But generally speaking, the correlation in life is between success and positive attitudes, not success and innate ability. I was talking recently with a man who told me an interesting story which relates to this point. He had always been successful in school, had been in all of the activities, had occupied leadership roles and, generally, everybody thought of him as a pretty bright person. He went on to college and experienced this same success. When he became a senior, he had a job working in the office of the dean, and one day accidentally came upon his own records and found, much to his surprise, that his ability was barely average. He said that for a while he was dumb-founded and didn't know what to do. He felt he had been living a lie and even felt guilty about his success. "Well," he said, "I had to decide to do something." So he said, "What I think I'll do is, since I've been fooling people all along, I'll just keep on trying to fool people as long as I can get away with it." Consequently, he went on through life, became a very successful businessman, a leader in his community, and at this time he is almost at retirement. He said, "You know, no one has found me out yet." You see, the point of this story is simply this: he had a positive attitude about himself and thereby experienced success. It is really fortunate that he didn't learn about his limited ability until he had already tasted the sweetness of success and had built enough self-confidence to go on. I have seen youngsters who were able to qualify for professional school when their ability was only average; but, you see, they didn't know that, and the fact that they didn't know permitted them to go on and operate at a very high level of success.

Question:

Well then, from what you say, our attitude about ourselves literally begins the day we are born.

Answer:

I would say it actually begins before we are born because the attitudes of our parents are transmitted to us through our environment. So if they are very positive people, we are going to be positive, too. Most of the attitudes of learners are developed before the age of five. If you get much beyond that point, you are really talking about modifying attitudes rather than developing the basic attitudes. That is why it is so important that the home environment promote a positive attitude.

Question:

Does the number of children that are in the family have much affect on attitudes? You know, we often hear about the middle-child syndrome and the only-child syndrome, for instance.

Answer:

Yes, this does make a difference. When a new child comes into a family, it is never the same family again because now it is a family with one more child. So, actually, the first child born into a family is most likely to get the most attention and has the best chance to develop—verbal skills, for example. When children come along after that, the parents have greater obligations, because there are more children, and they generally spend less time with each child. So, what we really need to do to build positive attitudes is to treat every child like an *only* child and make sure that we proportion our time so each one gets a sufficient amount to grow as an individual.

Question:

Can competition among children be healthy in a family?

Answer:

Yes, it can be healthy if the children always have the security of knowing that they are able to fail without losing approval. The only time that we will try anything new is if we realize that, if we try it and fail, it is not going to have a long-term negative effect for us. This is the kind of security we all need. It is helpful if each child has a special area in which to excel, separate from the interest areas of brother and sisters. This gives a feeling of individuality which is important and minimizes the comparison of accomplishments between siblings.

Question:

Don't we sometimes make a mistake by comparing an older child's grades or accomplishments to those of a younger child?

Answer:

Oh, absolutely. Each child should be treated as an individual, and those kinds of comparisons are not helpful. When you start drawing comparisons, there is bound to be one child who comes out on the short end and he is going to suffer because of it.

Question:

What are the effects of those things that are not really inside the home but around the home environment, such as the community? Are these important in developing attitudes?

Answer:

Oh yes, the *total* environment is what we must consider. So, the community in which we live, the church we attend, the people with whom we come in contact—all of these are important. It is crucial for parents to make sure there is positive input from all areas. It's important to know the children with whom your child plays. I wouldn't keep him away from other people because we grow and we learn and we develop in the socialization process, but I would want parents to make sure their children have the best possible social contacts. For example, if our children play with boys and girls who are a lot older, there is an opportunity, you see, for ours to become submissive. This is an example of the sort of thing we have to watch. My dad used to say, "Birds of a feather flock together." Don't permit yourself to be intimidated into letting your child play with children who chronically misbehave. You can't afford to have those attitudes absorbed.

Question:

There seems to be great disagreement in our nation today as to whether children should be punished—or perhaps I should say—how children should be disciplined. I take it, then, methods of discipline have a lot to do with attitudes developed by young children.

Answer:

Yes. This is one of the problem areas, too. When improper discipline procedures are used, they can mark and scar a child. I would like to take the broader term of discipline. As parents, we need to develop in our children attitudes of organization. Now, I don't mean "overorganization" where they become slaves to planning, but we need to teach them to take care of their obligations, to meet their deadlines, and to have

135

responsibilities in the home. An organized lifestyle will serve them well in school and beyond. When we do have to punish, it should be done in a positive way. When a child breaks a rule or does something that obviously can't be condoned, I would suggest to the parents that first, before they do any disciplining, to reinforce the love relationship by saying to the child, "I love you, and because I love you I'm going to have to do something about this situation." Then do it, and use the type of discipline that solves the matter quickly. I would much prefer that parents use corporal punishment—within reason, of course—rather than long-term anger or withholding of love and acceptance. Whatever the punishment, get it over with and then say, "Okay, now you've paid for what you've done. Everything is all right again and now we can move ahead." You see, it is that fresh, new start that we all need to keep us growing.

Question:

Isn't it true that, in many cases, parents object to disciplinary measures taken by the school? What should a parent do in such a situation?

Answer:

Conflict between teacher and parent really puts the child in the middle. I think if there is ever a question about the discipline that has been used, we as parents need to keep an open mind, talk with the teacher, and make sure we have all of the facts. Teachers are human beings and occasionally they make mistakes. But let's assume we are all working for the welfare of the child. Let's get together and let's not be adversaries, because if we are adversaries, the child is going to be the pawn.

Question:

If you have ever been on the steps of a school when it first opens, you see the tears that flow and the lingering parent who is hesitant to leave the child that first day. All of us want our children to be ready for school, of course. What are some of the considerations that we should keep in mind as we try to get our children prepared with the proper attitude for school?

Answer:

We need to prepare the child for *success* in school. We need to talk about how school is fun. We need to have him looking forward to it with anticipation, and we should never talk about bad things that might happen in school. It is like the parents who take the child to the dentist and keep saying things like: "This won't hurt you," or "It's not going to hurt." The word "hurt" stands out and the child builds an expectation of being hurt. When we talk about school, we need to emphasize the pleasantness of it—talk about the "fun" activities that they have there, how he is going to get to spend some time at school with other boys and girls and that afterward, he is going to come home to Mom and Dad. You see, home and school form a cycle of security. Don't treat school as an alienation from family. I know it is tough for moms and dads on that first day of kindergarten but, for the child's sake, we need to be optimistic, enthusiastic and happy. We should deliver the child to school, then go home and let the teachers, who know how to deal with this situation, take it from there.

Question:

We see in today's society a great emphasis upon athletics and athletic excellence. Sports participation can psychologically endanger a child. What do you suggest in this type of situation?

Answer:

I would not encourage team competition for very young children. I just don't think they are ready for it. There are many things they can do to help physical development, but team competition is not the best. The psychological danger is even greater. If you are in a situation where your child is going to participate in baseball or football at a very young age, I would hope that you not build up unreasonable expectations and criticize him when he makes a mistake. He is not ready for that. I would also be very careful about the person who works with him as a coach. The coach who knows how to prepare him for success *and* defeat, the one who reinforces his adequacy and his worth even though he is not doing well in a particular game or situation—this is what you want. It really concerns me when coaches have winning uppermost in mind when working with very young children—it's just not reasonable. We need to play the game for fun. Winning is certainly something we need to teach boys and girls to try to do but, at the same time, we must give them the security that, if they are defeated, we think no less of them.

Question;

In your experience over the many years you have been in education and dealing with many, many young people, what are some of the more frequent causes of poor attitudes among the students?

Answer:

Usually, with the child that comes from a home where there is conflict, where there is lack of love among family members, there is a scarring effect upon the child. Where one has been belittled and punished in the wrong way, where one does not have the basic security of love of family—this is a very hard thing for young people to deal with. The child who has been loved, been given attention, been made to feel completely adequate, the one who has not been given activities beyond his or her ability to perform— that's the child who is ready to go to work and really do well in school. Poor attitudes are inherited. If the parents have a low attitude about themselves and poor aspirations, this will be reflected in the child.

Question:

Television has been many things to many people. It has been called many things over the years—the boob tube, the magic box—whatever. Has television changed things for young people in one way or another?

Answer:

Yes, and I think it has made the job of parents much more difficult. To its credit, television has increased the ability of children to verbalize, so they come to school having much greater facility with the language than children once had. On the other side of the coin, there is also much on television today that will build negative attitudes in boys and girls. They see shows on television that emphasize the problems of life and the bad things which can happen to parents and all of us, and it tends to build up in them fears of what might happen in the future. I would think that parents would want to be very selective with what they have their children watch. Let them see shows that entertain them—ones that reinforce the positive things in life.

Question:

Are you recommending that teachers use television as a teaching aid in the classroom?

Answer:

Oh yes, I think television can be used as a teaching aid, but the teacher has to be selective in what she lets them see.

Question:

Would you summarize for parents what they can do to ensure proper attitudes in young people?

Answer:

Most important of all is the example that is lived in the home. You see, boys and girls learn much more from example than they ever learn from what we say. They need an example that emphasizes optimism— the positive things in life—and the hope there is in the world. Then I would say that next in importance is the atmosphere of obvious love. We need to use the word *love* — "I love you" — and we need to show it by our touching and our holding, the warmth we have for each other and by the giving of our time to children. No matter what we say, if we don't give our time to children, our lack of genuine concern will be obvious. The child knows we spend our time on the things we really value.

Then I would say consistency, so the child knows what to expect at all times—particularly in discipline. If the child knows the standards of the family and knows that if certain things are done there is going to be punishment, he can deal with that, but uncertainty can be traumatic, and this is another way of saying inconsistency. I would say also it is important not to have conflict in the presence of the child. The best thing would be for parents to agree and to get along all the time, but I'm sure that is unrealistic. If there are arguments or periods of conflict, these should not be done in the presence of the child. We should at least have the good judgment to have these conflicts off to ourselves and leave the child out of it—and certainly not make the child a part of it.

In addition, we need to let children have a feeling that they are contributing to the family. There is nothing that helps to build positive attitudes better than to feel that what we are doing is meaningful and important and helpful to other people. So, they should be assigned tasks of real importance—not just taking out the garbage. Responsibility for keeping their own rooms in order would be one thing, and performing other tasks that are in keeping with their maturity levels so that they all feel they are contributing to the welfare of everyone else. We should make sure that they are at the proper level of physical maturity for anything that is undertaken.

Don't push a youngster into school too soon. There is really no reason to. It would be much better to let him be more mature—for his learning to be easy—so that he can say to himself: "I'm good at this. I'm good at school work, and I'm always going to be." Putting a child into school too soon causes him to work closer to the frustration level and can cause a negative reaction such as feeling school is not really much fun. The same thing is true for other activities. I think that parents who cause their children to attempt physical activities requiring coordination that has not developed run a risk of building frustration and negativism. And I would say also, "Don't try to live out your dreams through your children." Many parents feel that they did not accomplish what they should have at some point in life and so they attempt to make up for that through their children. Children should be treated as individuals; they should have freedom to think and to choose for themselves. We need to love them enough to let them become increasingly independent.

Another important thing to remember is to help your children develop habits which will support them. Good habits really help—like the habit of simple planning before a task is begun. These things will carry them through, will serve them well, all through life. And then I would say finally, try to protect your children from trauma when they are very young. There is nothing to be gained by telling those real scary stories or letting them watch frightening television programs. Do not subject them to unnecessary trauma.

Question:

Speaking of that particular category, the scary stories and trauma, do you consider it unhealthy should a child from five to eleven or twelve suddenly run into bed with Mommy or Daddy because of some frightening experience?

Answer:

If that ever happens, for goodness sake put your arms around the child and hug him and console him because rejecting him at that point would be detrimental to him. It is well to look into what caused it, but at that moment provide security. A traumatic experience has lifelong repercussions. I recommend that parents not subject their very young children to such occasions as funerals. In certain family situations, that cannot be avoided, but we need to make sure that they have the comfort and the information to deal with something like that. Unnecessary exposure to trauma is not going to produce anything positive.

Question:

Some persons who are listening to our conversations may have children who are already evidencing negative feelings or unacceptable behavior. What should parents do in a situation like that?

Answer:

Then we are dealing with behavior modification, and this is often the case. Even if we try to do our best, there will be times when behavior is not exactly what we want it to be, and the child does not have the confidence that would be most beneficial. The best thing to do is to emphasize the positive. Instead of talking about the problem area—instead of emphasizing the things the child doesn't do well or can't do well—look at the areas that *are* going well. Look at the things the child can do and praise those things. There is an interesting phenomenon at work here. We have learned that emphasizing the problem areas seems to make the situation worse. It makes the sore spot more painful as we keep probing and rubbing at it. But if we start talking about the things that are going well, the positive things, as these areas grow even higher, the problem areas seem to improve. So there is little to be gained by talking about the things the child can't do or the things the child has done wrong; it's much better to talk about the things that are going right and emphasize the positive because this tends to bring more growth.

HOW CAN POSITIVE ATTITUDES
BE DEVELOPED IN SPECIAL EDUCATION
STUDENTS?

Question:

Dr. Fitzwater, when we are working with children who are in need of remedial help or special education, are the concepts for building positive attitudes appreciably different?

Answer:

Not really. Obviously we have to do something to compensate for the handicapping condition, whatever it is, but the same principles hold true. What the child thinks of himself is the most crucial aspect. Image, self-adequacy — anything we can do to enhance this will help the special education child just as any other child. We have seen children with some pretty severe handicaps do very well. If anything, the child in special education needs more concentration on building positive attitudes than others because self-images are so important. This child has a handicapping condition which he or she is gong to have to endure for a lifetime. A positive attitude is going to be the difference in living adequately and successfully or not.

Question:

What has been done in public schools to meet the needs of these children?

Answer:

Our track record was not good for a long time, and it is still pretty bad in many places. In the distant past, just about everything we did emphasized the handicap. We zeroed in and concentrated on the handicapping condition and we did not put the emphasis on strengths. All children, in special education or not, have many strengths. What we need to do is put our emphasis on the strengths. As these strengths grow stronger, children compensate for the handicapping condition. Modern programs of special education are doing a much better job of emphasizing positive strengths.

Question:

Should these special education children be separated, or should they be in classes with so-called "normal" children?

Answer:

Well, that depends. In some situations where the handicapping condition is very, very severe, such as with a severely retarded child, we may have to keep them in separate classes because the needs are so different. But even with the severely handicapped, we ought to try to have them together during lunch periods and recreational periods. These children need to learn to live in the world of normal people. If the handicapping condition is not very severe, then I would opt for the so-called "mainstreaming" which is being done more and more today. In this way, we keep all children together and then we do something to help handicapped children keep up with the regular children. For example, a child who is minimally handicapped can be kept in the regular classroom, and special teachers can be brought in to help so that he can keep up.

Question:

In our previous discussion, you seemed to speak in favor of having children stay in the home until kindergarten age. Is the situation any different when you are talking about handicapped children?

Answer:

Yes, it could be. An early start seems to be a very crucial thing in dealing with children with special needs. I would think, though, that we ought to keep the handicapped child in the home except for those periods when he or she is getting special help with the handicapping condition. The security and the warmth of the home are just as necessary for the special education child as any other, maybe even more so.

Question:

Many of our schools today have special teachers who work with children who need remedial education but who are not severely handicapped. Is this really doing the job?

Answer:

I think we are getting better all the time. We have leared to accentuate the positive. We have learned to give the children activities which will build their psychological strength, and this is helping. The main change, though, is that we no longer concentrate on learning problems. We concentrate on strengths, and we try to help the child grow from wherever he or she is. It does no good to emphasize that the child is behind normal children — he knows that already, so this is negative and detrimental. The growth should be highlighted, however minimal it may be.

Question:

How good is the identification process of accurately pinpointing the children who need special help?

Answer:

It's getting better. The group identification procedures that we used some years ago are questionable, at best. When it comes to identifying a child for special education, we need to use individual testing devices; we have to make sure that we are not making a mistake. Years ago, we captured children in special education who really had cultural differences or poverty syndromes. The children so identified thought of themselves as handicapped children and the world responded to the cues. As a result, they became special education children when they really didn't have handicaps at all.

Question:

I sense from some of the remarks you've made that we haven't been very positive in dealing with handicapped children. Do our attitudes have to be very different when we are talking about various types of handicaps, or should we more or less have the same positive attitude toward all of them?

Answer:

I think the positive attitude is the key, no matter what the type of handicap—whether it is blindness, deaf-

145

ness, mental retardation, or whatever. We need to go as far as we can with every child, and that's the secret to the positive approach. We take the child wherever we find him and we move him ahead just as far as we can possibly go. In the case of a child who is blind, we try to develop strengths in the other areas, such as hearing, and compensate by having braille instruction and similar helps to make up for the handicapping condition. But we emphasize the positive and try as much as possible to ignore the negative. That is the key to causing the most growth. We are all handicapped to some degree and we all have strengths.

Question:

Does the fact that someone is physically handicapped always mean that he will be psychologically or mentally handicapped as well?

Answer:

Oh, no. A lot of children who have physical handicaps grow up to be successful adults who have a lot of self-confidence. Some of our best motivational speakers at conferences and conventions are handicapped people who tell how they succeeded in spite of their handicap. In a sense, the handicap caused them to succeed. It got their attention. It caused them to work harder and compensate by developing other strengths. I think this illustrates what we are talking about. The child who is blind can develop other senses to a very high degree and, if the attitude is right, only the severest of handicaps can prevent success and happiness in the truly determined person.

Question:

What are some suggestions that you have for parents and teachers in working with remedial or special education students?

Answer:

The first thing we should talk about is prevention. For example, inoculation of women of childbearing age for measles would prevent so many children from suffering handicaps. I think early identification is another key. We have to have parents and teachers

146

sensitive to spotting handicaps so that we can get to work on the problem early. Then I would advise that the people around the handicapped child look at their own attitudes. It is crucial that we be very positive and provide an environment of security—one that helps the child grow rather than the reverse. We have to be honest and we have to be realistic. The sooner we get parents to realize they are going to have to rear a handicapped child, the better. If the situation is real, then let's get to work and do something about it. We need to provide as much normalcy as possible for the child. We don't want to rub the sore spot and make it more painful by talking about it all the time. The more that children with handicapping conditions can be put into normal activities, the more normal they will become. Our goal should be as much of a normal environment as possible.

WHAT IS THE TEACHER'S ROLE IN BUILDING POSITIVE ATTITUDES?

Question:

Dr. Fitzwater, is the teacher's role in developing proper attitudes appreciably different from that of a parent?

Answer:

Only to this extent: the teacher comes into the picture at a much later period. Many attitudes have been developed to a very high degree; in fact, *most* attitudes have been developed. The teacher has to deal more with behavior modification than the development of the basic attitudes; but, beyond that, the two are pretty much the same. Children learn what they live, so in the school as in the home, children who live in a positive environment develop positive attitudes. Unfortunately the reverse is also true. And I might add, parenthetically: Children learn far more from the way a teacher behaves than what he or she teaches formally.

Question:

Are teachers generally given special training to help them do the best job in teaching positive attitudes?

Answer:

Professional schools vary but all teachers take some psychology. Generally, though, such training is at a minimal level. It's interesting that teachers tend to teach more the way they were taught than the way they were taught to teach. I think there is still a great need today for in-service training for teachers as we reinforce the obligation of a teacher to motivate and accentuate the positive. I'm concerned when I hear teachers say something like: "Well, the students who come to my class don't seem to want to learn mathematics." The truth is learners are not supposed to come to class wanting to learn. The first job of any teacher is to motivate, to turn the children on to the subject area—that's fundamental. I can remember

148

some years ago a youngster going off to college, and this youngster was going to study law. Much to his chagrin, right at the beginning of his undergraduate years, he found that he was faced with a four-credit course in geology. He had no previous interest in geology and he was quite negative about this. Two or three weeks later, I ran into that same young man and all he wanted to talk about was geology. He was really "turned on," and to this day it is an abiding interest of his. You see, that teacher had recognized the first obligation of every teacher—to inspire the students to be interested in learning his subject area. We must keep reinforcing the idea that teachers are teaching students, not subjects. The atmosphere which reassures the child is absolutely essential. Kids must feel their teacher is their advocate— someone to whom they can turn for help and comfort.

Question:

You mention that teachers should "turn kids on." How do you accomplish this?

Answer:

Basically, it's a job of inspiration and a disciplined approach to teaching. We usually think of discipline as punishment, but there is also this side to discipline: Students need to be organized so they can see the logic of studying a given course, and they need help to perform in such a way that they get satisfaction from it. Here again, the positive emphasis is so very, very important. If the teacher starts the beginning of the year by talking about all the things that the students will not be allowed to do, and makes up long lists of rules and this sort of thing, that's emphasizing the negative. I would much rather see a teacher at the beginning of the year get the students down to work quickly. She tells them what has to be accomplished and how they are going to work together this year to do it. She says something like: "I'm going to let you help me with planning some of these activities so that they will be the most to your liking. We have a lot to do, but working together, we are going to get it done."

With this positive emphasis at the beginning of the year, the students are more likely to get down to work and, incidentally, when they get busy, they have less time to think about things that might get them into trouble. The students respond to the cue of the teacher. She makes sure she gives a cue which brings a positive response. Some students, of course, because of special needs, may have behavior problems which have to be approached on a diagnostic basis. But generally speaking, the strong motivation at the beginning will remove much of the need for behavior modification later on.

Question:

Does the grading system get in the way of building positive attitudes? We have become accustomed to certain things such as the old ABC-type of grading system, and parents have a negative reaction to new grading systems. Will grading systems have to be changed to make schools more positive?

Answer:

Parents react negatively to new grading systems, generally speaking, because they don't understand them. You see, most of us grew up with the ABC system, and even though it conveys virtually no information to the parents, we still feel we understand it and we feel comfortable with it. When a new grading system is proposed, we think all sorts of things. We may think that the old values that we hold so dear are being minimized or that school is becoming too easy or the teachers lackadaisical, that discipline is suffering. There is seldom any truth to such fears. Schools are trying to come up with a system which conveys information parents need. At the same time, while conveying this information, they are trying not to create negative attitudes because this is far more important than the grading ever will be. Report cards do far more harm than good. They are for the convenience of parents who can't, or won't, take the time to learn how their children are performing. We'd be better off without them.

Question:

In view of that, doesn't there seem to be too much emphasis placed on grades in schools today?

Answer:

Absolutely, and I wish I knew some way to get around it. Any time you attempt to minimize grades in any way, you get quite a reaction from the community because of lack of understanding. But the emphasis on grades puts children in unwholesome competition at an early age, and it causes them to put more concern into the grades than the actual learning that they are getting out of school. It is something we haven't solved. We need to work on it, and I would encourage parents to be cooperative with teachers when new grading systems are tried. You see, we must communicate information about achievement —a grade of C doesn't tell us anything. If I took my annual physical and the doctor gave me a C, what would that tell me? My liver might be A and my heart an F—the average would be C but I'd be dead.

Question:

Well, that leads to this next question. We also group students according to their ability in the classroom. Does this have implications for learner attitude?

Answer:

That's another controversy, and it's another situation that has great implication for attitude development. I once worked with a school district that was just about ready to explode over the business of ability grouping.

Over the years, you see, they had developed a system of grouping students according to their ability, even in the early grades of elementary school. They had one class of all-very-bright students, several groups of average or slightly below average, and then they had a slow group. The children were in these classes all day long. Over the years, the teachers with the greatest tenure were the ones who taught all the bright classes. The very new teachers, who had the least experience, had to teach the low classes. The results were disastrous because all poor kids were together, classes were racially segregated, and it was generally an unnatural situation. This was a time bomb that was "defused" just in time. I personally lean toward heterogeneous grouping, with subgrouping to take care of individual differences in learning. For example, the students in fifth grade are placed into home-rooms heterogeneously but then go to ability groups at various times during the day for instructional purposes. In that way, the children experience a real-life environment where people are different but also get advantage of competition. They also have a chance to learn leadership, incidentally, and they have an opportunity at the same time to work at their particular level in a given subject area. You know, in a class that has all very bright students or all very slow students, some very disturbing things can happen. In the bright group, where all students have leadership ability potential, many are frustrated because there can only be so many leaders. In the slower group you have lack of leadership but the most profound thing is the image the learners get of themselves. I can remember the situation vividly where a young man had been in a strictly homogeneous situation. The school changed and went to heterogeneous grouping, and the first day of school he walked into his new class, looked around, and he said, "Hey, I'm in the wrong class, Teacher. I'm supposed to be with the dummies." Well, that shows you the kind of aspirations that youngster had. In a slow group, the learners' expectations fall; as expectations fall, performance will fall.

Question:

Then it is true that grading and grouping can cause great psychological and motivational problems for students.

Answer:

Absolutely. We need to have grading systems and grouping systems that give positive reinforcement rather than negative reinforcement. It is heartbreaking to see a youngster go into first grade and feel good about himself until the report cards come out and self-image is crushed. He gets C's, maybe even D's. When the report is taken home and the parents say, "Oh, you are not doing well, you're not very smart," that kid says to himself: Hey, I just learned something. I'm not very smart, so I'm going to act like that the rest of my life.

Question:

Would a similar feeling come from a child being placed in special education?

Answer:

Yes, it could. This is why we don't want to separate special education children from others. You will hear a lot about mainstreaming in the future, as we try to solve the problem of stigmatizing children.

Question:

Are there any particular critical periods, as the young person grows, where self-images need particular nurturing?

Answer:

Yes, they need nurturing at every level, but there are certain key places where parents and the school should give extra care. Preschool, which is largely the domain of the parents, is a critical period. The basic values and opinions about oneself—basic images— are developed there. Then, at entrance into school. This is why kindergarten teachers and first-grade teachers have to be specially trained to recognize the importance of early success in school. The children tend to perform throughout life the way they do in the beginning. There is another critical period, too. That is the period of adolescense. Young people going through this period already have plenty of problems, and it's a time when attitudes are modified to a great degree. It is one of the few times in life when we make real dramatic changes. Much reinforcement is needed during adolescence. There is already a feeling on the part of the children that they should be gaining independence and pulling away from the parents. So, parents will need to reach out at this time and be very sensitive to these changes and handle the situation in an appropriate way.

Question:

We have talked about grading. How about standardized testing?

Answer:

The same thing is true with standardized testing. We test too much, and much of the testing we do is not used. Then when we do test, we tend to use it for the wrong purpose. Standardized testing should be for decision making at the school district level. It should be for curriculum modification. But we tend to give standardized tests, and then we report the results to the parents and the children and what happens? Whatever we report, the child takes it as gospel and starts to perform in keeping with that. There have been all sorts of experiments along this line. Some years ago, one principal gave teachers distorted test scores. He put real high scores with some of the students who were really not nearly that smart, and teacher expectations rose based on the test scores and what happened? The kids started to perform like bright children. The danger is that we lower aspirations by telling students that they are below average or slow—they will usually accept this and perform accordingly. The whole labeling business is a problem area, and I would recommend to teachers and schools that they use as few labels as possible. I'm embarrassed to admit it, but there was a time when I sincerely believed that unless students received at least 120 on their I.Q. test, they should not be allowed to pursue French in the junior high school. Some years later when I made my first trip to Paris, to my amazement, I suddenly realized that all boys and girls could learn to speak French because all the children there did— even the mentally retarded spoke French. They were expected to and they responded to that expectation.

Question:

What types of personalities of teachers do the best job in building positive attitudes in learners?

Answer:

You framed that question exactly right because the personality of the teacher does have a profound effect. The teacher who has a genuine love of people, the teacher who is turned on to her subject which she is teaching, the one who is positive in discipline methods, the one who uses a grading system that is also positive—there are the kinds of things that we need. Then, teachers should avoid labeling students. We need to teach students rather than subjects and there is a difference. Some teachers, unfortunately, have their subject set up before the students ever arrive, and they go ahead and teach as if the learners really made no difference at all. Of course, we know this is not true. The teacher who is genuine and not "put on" is the one who is necessary in building positive attitudes. The teacher who is compassionate and has high standards is the teacher we go back to see years after we get out of school. You see, the two of them go together. The teacher who is compassionate, who avoids tension and anxiety and things which produce these conditions, is a positive teacher.

We should operate in such a way that students know where they stand every minute. For example, a grade should never be a surprise. If the kind of communication is going on that is really necessary for security and warmth in the classroom, grades won't come as a surprise. We mentioned earlier that parents should be consistent in the way in which they deal with children. Exactly the same thing is true with teachers. Teachers who are consistent help students feel secure and comfortable. Certainly teachers should not be rigid. If you ever hear of a grading system where someone missed an A because an A was 94 and the student had 93⅞, well you see, that is ridiculous. Our grading systems are not that precise. I think a good rule for teachers to live by is: if you are going to make a mistake, make it in favor of the child.

Question:

So what you are saying, then, is that a teacher who brings out the positive in young people is a very human and loving person.

Answer:

Yes, I think that is certainly true. The teacher who is enthusiastic tends to bring about enthusiasm in learners. The teacher who is optimistic tends to have optimistic learners. As to genuineness, the teacher who is comfortable in her own skin, who feels good about herself, radiates these habits and attitudes to the students in the classroom. I like teachers who are real advocates of children, who don't fear children, who aren't defensive with children—these are the ones who seem to do the best job and have the least trouble in controlling children. Children are human and understanding with us, too. If they know *we* are trying to do the right thing, they respond to our cues and they will do the right thing as well.

WHAT CAN BE DONE TO ASSIST GIFTED LEARNERS?

Question:

Dr. Fitzwater, we have discussed normal children and we have discussed children who are in special education. Are there any particular considerations that we ought to think about when we are dealing with the very bright, or gifted, student?

Answer:

Yes. I think, first of all, we need to remember the admonition that fertile soil will grow weeds just as readily as flowers. I often say to parents when they have a gifted child, "You are in an envied position; but, as with most envied positions, it brings a lot of challenges."

Question:

What are the statistics on bright children and success in life?

Answer:

The facts about bright children are somewhat sobering. We need to remember that not all bright children succeed. Of the bright children who are in the same classes all the way through school, some will succeed; others will become dropouts. So just being bright does not absolutely ensure success. Intellect is probably one of the items of less importance when it comes to success and happiness. There are other things much more important. Ease of learning in the early years can build a readiness for failure. If things come too easily, the youngster comes to expect that everything in life is going to be easy in all areas and this is unrealistic. There are more bright children among the mentally ill than persons of average ability or less than average ability, so it is important to put brightness in perspective. If we behave properly around the very bright child, then everything will usually turn out happily. But I have known many situations where parents didn't react properly and the outcome was very bad.

Question:

Where, then, is the correlation if it is not between brightness and success?

Answer:

The high correlation is between *attitude* and success, not brightness and success. Here again, it it what the person thinks of himself. If you are bright and have a good image, that's fine. But also, if you are average and have a good self-image, you can be very successful. It is the attitude which plays the large role in success.

Question:

Suppose the parents of a bright child were to ask you what to do about their own personal situation. What are some of the guidelines which should be followed for greater success?

Answer:

Well, let me share with you a couple of case studies, and these are based on fact. We can see how two bright children came out because of the way they behaved and the way others behaved around them. In Situation A, there was a youngster who found early in life that learning came very easily. The child learned spontaneously; he was able to read long before he entered school. Well, this ease of learning in the early years lured the child and the parents into complacency. The child became braggadocious and so did the parents. They had unrealistic expectations of the school. They felt that just because the child was bright that everyone in the school ought to cater to their needs at all times. The parents became hyper-critical of the school and indeed the whole environment. They started planning college even before the child was out of first grade; and really what they were doing, they were ignoring short-term goals that are necessary to reach long-term goals. As you can imagine, the outcome of this situation was bad. The child became isolated from other children. Instead of achieving the social development which all children need, this child withdrew because it wasn't fun to be with other people. The parents saw no need for things like sports or physical education, and spoke openly against them. So instead of this child turning out to be well-rounded, he became socially and physically retarded, emotionally distorted, bitter, and withdrawn. The outcome of that situation was very bad. Now let me give you another situation. This was a child of very gifted ability, but the parents kept it in perspective. They reinforced the student in the intellectual and physical areas by positive statements. They said things like: "I'm glad that reading is such fun for you and that it is easy. You'll always find reading to be fun." If the classes in school didn't seem challenging, the parents supplemented them. But they weren't critical of the school and they didn't become negative. They taught the child how to play with those who didn't learn as fast. After all, bright people need to learn to get along in the world the way it is; not everyone is bright. Instead of keeping the child away from others, they made sure that she had opportunities to be with other children. They taught her leadership skills. They made sure that her physical development was not overlooked. In this instance, brightness was made a blessing and not an impediment.

Question:

What type of programs should schools offer for bright children?

Answer:

Basically, the programs should be about the same as for other children, with additional opportunities for the child who gets through the regular work quickly. Rather than making it a totally different environment by isolating the bright child, I would say the secret is to supplement what goes on in the regular classroom so that the youngster has an opportunity to use his full ability. The most important thing, though, will be the way the parents react. If they give positive reinforcement, the child will be able to take brightness in stride.

Question:

It sounds as though parents' attitudes are more

important than anything else. Specifically, what should parents do?

Answer:

First of all, relax. Don't become so tense and think that this is a challenge that you have to think about every minute. And I would say, secondly, make sure that you help the school develop the total child. If the child learns very easily, then maybe you should put most of your efforts into other areas, such as physical development. Make sure you work with your teachers; they see the child in a more objective way. And I would say this, too: perseverance should be a learning goal for bright children. The bright child learns so easily that he doesn't have to learn things like perseverance just to get by. But later on in life, there are going to be other challenges where he will have to learn to "hang tough" — as the kids say. So I say to parents: Help your children learn perseverance. Teach them the value of hard work. Give them tasks to do outside of the area of intellectual endeavors. Give them other tasks to do so that they can learn the good feeling that comes from a job well done. Teach your children leadership skills. They have the ability to be leaders. With a little help, they can learn to be positive leaders and help other people. Teach them skills which will gain rapport with other children—all children. And teach them tact so that they don't lord it over others just because they have more ability.

Question:

Should bright children start school early to get a head start?

Answer:

Generally, I would say no. I see very little to be gained by that. If the child has an adequate home where enriching experiences can be given, I would say no. The danger in starting school early is that the physical and emotional maturity will not be adequate to deal with the situation. And instead of getting ahead of the game, we incur scars—social and emotional scars—which actually minimize the brightness that the child has.

Question:

Are there particular periods in the development of the bright child that are especially crucial?

Answer:

Yes, at the beginning. When he starts school, it's very important that the child learn to live in the environment without unrealistic expectations or without the feeling that he or she is appreciably different. He needs to learn to get along. The period of adolescence is another crucial period. That is where the children will call the bright ones "egg head" unless they have learned the social skills, unless they participate in all the activities of the school so that they are not so different. So before school starts, the early years of school, the adolescence period—these would be the most crucial times.

Question:

Let me see if I understand this correctly. If a person is particularly bright, there are probably other areas of development that need more attention than the intellectual areas.

Answer:

That's exactly right. I think this is obvious and it is so often overlooked by parents. If they have a bright child, they want him to work in the intellectual area, the reading area, the mathematics area, all the time. This is already the area of life that the child finds easiest, but it may not be true that this same child is able to keep up with peers when it comes to physical activities or anything else. So I think we need to look to rounding the child. We need to make sure that these other areas are developed because they are crucial to success and happiness and normalcy. I wish that parents who have bright children would give major attention to areas which don't develop spontaneously.

Question:

We often hear about the bright child being bored in the regular classroom programs. What would you say to this?

Answer:

I'd say to parents: Let your child run at the front of the pack instead of just being at the back of the pack and frustrated, trying to keep up all of the time. When children are double-promoted or accelerated unnaturally in school, they have trouble keeping up in the physical and emotional areas and, indeed, sometimes they are promoted to the point that, even though they are bright, they have trouble keeping up with their school work. I would much rather the child stay with the regular group and be given supplemental activities. At the same time he should learn leadership skills and learn to use the brightness for something more than just keeping up with school work. The child who parents think is bored is often spoiled by those parents who see an opportunity to satisfy their own ego needs through this type of criticism.

Question:

In discussing the topic of children who need special education, you mentioned that there were certain areas that were more critical than others. Is this also true in the case of the bright students?

Answer:

Yes, just as in our conversation a few minutes ago when we were talking about rounding the child, the point that needs to be stressed is that the child who is very bright tends to want to stay with the books. This is fine and we don't want to discourage it at all. We want to be positive by saying, "Oh, it's wonderful that you love books," "Here are more books." At the same time, we should not let the child hibernate with books and isolate himself from the rest of the world because this is an unnatural situation. We also need to be sure these children have a high opinion of their school. If we are critical of the school, if we say, "Well, you are bright and you are not getting what you should in school," the child will develop negative feelings toward school. There is nothing gained by teaching the child that something is wrong with his school. Even if it were true, there is nothing to be gained by it. As parents, we need to work on that sort of thing, but we certainly don't need to put that obligation on the child. We also need to emphasize to this youngster his obligations to family, to church, and whatever activities he might have. Being bright doesn't mean being able to disregard his responsibilities and get by with breaking rules. He must live up to his obligations, and it's much better when they're learned early. Praise needs to be given to him in areas other than merely learning from books, too. A child tends to repeat the things we praise, so if we just compliment him on his school work, the other areas will be let go, and that is not going to be best for the child in the long run.

APPENDIX II

TWO PROPOSALS FOR HUMANIZING EDUCATION

Proposal 1: Modify the Fact-centered Curriculum

Proposal 2: Minimize the College-prep High School

MODIFY THE FACT-CENTERED CURRICULUM

Education in America is determined more by a reaction to external stimuli than by developments within the profession. The thrust of education in different periods of history can be seen as educators tried to reorient the status quo to serve the changing needs of society. Thus, the pendulum of emphasis shifts in response to wars and other dramatic social changes rather than in response to newly discovered knowledge as is generally the case in other professions.

We had life-adjustment education in the 1930's because the Great Depression indicated that people could succeed best in sustaining themselves if they understood their environment and their relationship to other people. Unfortunately, John Dewey is both credited and maligned as the author of life adjustment. The truth is that his ideas would never have taken hold had it not been for the dramatic effects of the depression, so this controversial philosophy of education persisted until the needs of World War II made it apparent that people had to know how to perform specific skills. Subsequently, life-adjustment education, with its nonacademic stress, gave way to a concentrated academic curriculum.

After the war, the fact-centered curriculum grew with the aid of the standardized testing movement, which also stressed the mastery of facts. With the advent of Sputnik and the age of space exploration, the philosophy was extended so that we have now adopted a fact-centered curriculum to the virtual exclusion of other important emphases.

There is nothing inherently wrong with a strong emphasis on facts. In the training of teachers, for example, this stress has had a good effect. While teachers once completed their entire education with very little study in a content area, there exists now a wholesome trend toward the mastery of subject matter in a given field. The stress on facts within the public schools, however, can become too great.

While the prestige of the fields of hard science and mathematics has risen to almost holy status, that of the humanities has been diminished. Judgments as to the worth of a particular subject tend to be made more upon its contribution to technical advances than to progress in humanitarian pursuits. The pendulum has swung so far that we are now obsessed with facts and giving too little concern to such things as the learning of values, the appreciation of the American heritage and the development of skills in human relationships.

In attempting to make a case for a change, it is well to bear in mind that no one is proposing a de-emphasis of the three R's of education. The fundamental skills of communication and computation should be thoroughly taught in the elementary grades and extended throughout secondary school. The change that is needed is to balance the secondary curriculum so that it produces graduates who have an interest in, and skill for, attacking the major problems of today and the unanticipated problems of the future.

When we look at the courses taken by the majority of today's students, we get the feeling that an attempt is being made to teach them everything that they will need to know throughout their lifetime. Such a goal is ridiculous! In a world that changes as rapidly as ours, how can we ever hope to give young people all the answers they will need when we cannot identify the questions that are going to require answers? Who can tell what our world will be like thirty years from now, or even ten years from now? We should be training young people for life in the twenty-first century instead of trying to teach them everything there is to know at this particular point in time.

Let us look at the current world leaders in science, industry, or in other pursuits. Could they have possibly learned everything they needed to know when they were in high school? Obviously not; they are leaders because of their ability to meet changing conditions. They can develop new understandings because of their frame of mind—the outlook which helps them to make new discoveries.

This is what we should be attempting to do in education today. We should be teaching young people how to meet new problems and solve them for themselves. We should give them basic values and behavior patterns so they can get along with other people. We should stimulate their curiosity and help them become independent learners. In this way, when new challenges arise in the future, they will not reach back for solutions that have been given to them in school. They will, instead, set about to develop a solution equal to the times.

This is why we should emphasize independent study instead of complete reliance upon the self-contained classroom and the lecture method of teaching. We would better serve our youth if we built large resource centers with information available for the students to research for themselves. In this way, we will build into them the habit of seeking information to solve problems. Thus, they will learn to master the *techniques* of research and exploration so that new solutions can be developed based upon a reservoir of knowledge and experience of the past. A student who can only regurgitate facts learned by unthinking repetition will not do well in an independent situation—which will be most characteristic of the needs of the future.

Teachers must become leaders of research activities so that they can help rather than hinder young people as they become independent learners. There is no question that this calls for a higher degree of skill on the part of the teacher, who actually becomes a director of new learning activities in this kind of environment. Of course, the teacher who cannot function unless the children are lined up row-by-row within four classroom walls will not be comfortable with independent study techniques. Principals who are not used to having people move freely about the building will also be uncomfortable in this setting.

It is obvious that a lot of retraining will be needed for teachers now in service, and much rearrangement of thinking will be necessary on the part of school board members and parents. This new education looks different from the old fact-centered curriculum. Now, students move forth from the schools into the community for part of their research, and they begin to question and challenge their leaders as they seek logical answers to their questions. Since changes can become annoying to those who resist change, it would be completely logical to expect backlashes to develop on the part of the profession and the community at large unless there is complete understanding of the new emphasis.

There are additional reasons for a need to modify the fact-centered curriculum. The great problems existing in the world today do not stem from a lack of knowledge in science and technology. In fact, these are the areas where we have made the greatest advances. We have put men on the moon and made other accomplishments of almost equal magnitude. In contrast, the ability of human beings to get along together has progressed very little. Man's inhumanity to man continues; factions in our pluralistic society battle with each other to the detriment of all. Hunger and poverty stalk the earth as its peoples struggle to maintain life for an exploding population. The question of survival looms not only for the individual but for all humankind.

169

The schools must produce people who can deal with problems for which there are no easy solutions. To do this we must develop within young people the attitude that all areas of learning are important. We must provide time in the curriculum for students to address themselves to all major concerns—scientific and humanitarian. We must give our future scientists an opportunity to study the humanities so that their training will not be so extremely narrow.

There is another trend that we need to change, too. There is a great movement away from the teaching of values in the public schools because of a fear that in doing so we will step on individual rights or interfere with prerogatives of the home. While I would agree that we should not teach dogma, a particular political persuasion or religious belief, there is still a great need to emphasize to young people the importance of reverence for life and a healthy respect for our national heritage. In doing this, we must not be hypocritical and gloss over our problems and mistakes of the past. At the same time, we must make young people aware of the achievements of our country and its commitment to the betterment of humanity.

The next generation may decide to change our republic substantially. Therefore, it is our duty—and our challenge—to ensure that a complete understanding of the past is part of the data upon which the change is based.

MINIMIZE THE COLLEGE-PREP HIGH SCHOOL

The American high school began as an academic, college-preparatory institution intended to provide the classical education needed for entrance into the colleges which, in turn, trained young men for the professions. Since, in those early days, young people did not need a high school education unless they were going to college, this kind of emphasis could be justified; the concept of secondary education for all youth was neither a national nor local objective.

The situation changed dramatically, though, in the twentieth century, particularly during the period after World War I and the Great Depression. Increased technology plus a growing humanitarianism placed greater emphasis upon maximum development of *all* people, thus giving rise to the concept of secondary education for all.

Today, the theory is even more defensible; yet, illogically, the typical American high school continues to function primarily as a college preparatory school, with little or no emphasis on the type of education that is required for the majority of students. Statistics show that about eighty per cent of the children who begin school will graduate from a senior high school—a number which has risen dramatically since the pre-World War II years, when only twenty per cent went that far. Moreover, of that eighty per cent now graduating, approximately half will enter college and only half of *those* students will earn a baccalaureate degree. So, in the final analysis, *only twenty per cent of our young people will actually graduate from a college or university.*

Why, then, should our high schools be overwhelmingly slanted to serve the needs of college-bound students? Would it not make more sense to have a balanced program leaning toward the needs of those who will graduate directly into the world of work?

Those students who are intellectually capable and who have the means and motivation to go to college will find that they can get a high school education that meets their needs. Another small percentage, perhaps eight per cent, will find that there are vocational programs available which teach the skills necessary to learn a trade, but the remaining students (as much as fifty per cent) take a conglomeration of courses which prepares them for nothing! They must take further training in technical schools or they will be unprepared for any specific vocation. One student recently put it aptly when he said that he felt that he was just collecting stamps so he could get his book filled and qualify for a diploma-even though there was nothing his diploma would get for him. He was probably right.

Why has the high school not changed to keep pace with the changing needs of society? The reasons are many and closely allied to the reasons why public schools have not made other changes that are necessary and reasonable.

Parent Attitude

The dream of a college education is firmly embedded in the makeup of our national mind. Those of us who have gone to college feel it would be a setback if our children did not. For those who have not had a college education, it is natural and commendable to want their children to have advantages they did not enjoy. These expectations pressure young people into entering a college-preparatory program even though statistics tell us that all children will not go on to college.

Cost

Academic education costs a lot less than vocational education. College-prep courses are generally taught in an all-purpose classroom which requires little more than desks, a chalkboard and four walls. Preparing students for the business world requires machinery such as typewriters, lathes, and calculators. Training of an auto mechanic or a refrigeration mechanic requires large areas, expensive equipment and small learning groups. The cost per child is easily twice that of a regular class.

Lack of Teachers

Not many aspiring teachers train in vocational fields. The colleges do not have facilities to train these teachers any more than high schools have laboratories to train vocational students. Moreover, we do not allow persons other than college graduates to teach them. Expert mechanics with garage-proven capabilities and television repairmen who have run a successful business are not permitted to teach in public school! Whereas some teacher-licensing agencies are gradually changing their positions in this regard, it is still a general rule that one has to have a college education plus a highly developed skill to teach a trade.

172

Resistance within the Educational Profession

Professional educators—teachers and administrators alike—tend to resent vocational education, and teachers in this field are held in low esteem compared to academic teachers. The fact that the profession has not been open to highly qualified people without college training is ample evidence that there is no thrust from within the profession to change this picture. Education is thought of as a white-collar job and will remain so unless something is done to change this kind of thinking.

There are many creative approaches in which to deal with the biases within the profession, the cost of vocational training and the reluctance on the part of parents and students to take these courses. The following is an example of how one community made great strides in solving this problem without violating any of the objections heretofore mentioned:

The community that we will describe is an industrial town of approximately 40,000 residents in which there was a shortage of skilled technicians. At the same time, high school graduates were finding it hard to get work. For example, a local hospital was critically short of people to work as nurse's aides, hospital custodians, laboratory technicians and licensed vocational nurses. Many of the students at the local high school would have been pleased to have a career in any of these vocations if they had been given the proper training.

The school is a typical, academically oriented high school. A follow-up study of the graduates has shown that about forty per cent enter college. Another ten per cent are in good vocational programs, but the remaining fifty per cent drop out of school or receive an array of unrelated courses until they accumulate enough to graduate.

When the community and educational leaders realized that the high school program was out of touch with student needs, school and student committees were formed to devise ways of solving the problem. The major thrust of their effort was to solve the dilemma of the fifty per cent, but they also recognized a related problem concerning those in the existing vocational classes who were receiving training on inefficient and outdated equipment. First, it was thought that a tremendous extension of vocational offerings would be the answer. When the cost of the new equipment and building was estimated, it was realized that neither enough money nor teaching staff was available to implement this approach.

The chosen alternative was to institute a large cooperative-education program, which would permit a student to take academic work at the high school on a half-day basis while working part-time in a local business establishment. This was coordinated by a school-community steering committee to ensure that it became an educational program in the finest sense and not just a way for students to get out of school to work part-time. A meaningful sequence of skills was determined for each trade area, and the school and business people coordinated their efforts very closely. Community leaders were glad to hire the needed workers whom they hoped to persuade to remain in their small hometown. School people were pleased because now they could provide up-to-date training for the young people and still not violate what they knew to be practical education.

The solution had many advantages:

1. An almost infinite variety of trades and skills became available to students.

2. Actual working conditions were made a part of the learning experience.

3. Students who had been dropping out of school because of financial need were now able to "earn and learn." Others without financial need took pride in their work because they were making a salary. (The school's public relations were tremendously enhanced by this high-level community involvement.)

4. Vast vocational offerings were made available at no extra cost to the schools. Even the salaries of the coordinators were not affected, since the students would have been in the classroom had they not been on the job.

5. The students who worked part-time graduated with actual work experience which made it easier to find a pemanent job. In fact, many of the students became full-time company employees after they graduated.

6. Parent cooperation was good since the students could take either vocational or precollege courses in addition to the work experience.

The case could easily be made that *all* young people would benefit from the experience of actually holding a job before they graduate from high school. It would not only give them a greater perspective of real life, but it would help them learn the importance of getting along with people and generally enhance their knowledge, contributing to their maturity.

If the academic program of a particular high school should preclude the implementation of any other during the regular school year, it would still behoove the administrators and community leaders to structure some kind of work-experience training during the summer. Even if the students did not receive a salary, they would still benefit from the experience.

Would a program in cooperative education discourage students from planning a college education? This has not been found to be true. The sincerely determined college-bound student finds his appreciation for the college opportunity enhanced with the knowledge of the realities of the workaday world. Those who do not intend to pursue a higher education with eagerness and a great deal of effort are probably not going to succeed in such an environment, anyway.

OTHER PUBLICATIONS
by
Ivan W. Fitzwater, Ed.D.

BOOKS
Finding Time for Success and Happiness
You Can Be a Powerful Leader

AUDIO CASSETTE PROGRAMS
BUILDING POSITIVE ATTITUDES IN LEARNERS
CONQUERING STRESS AND TENSION
HOW TO IMPROVE STUDENT ACHIEVEMENT
IVAN FITZWATER IN POETRY AND PROSE
IVAN FITZWATER ON STAGE
THE TIME OF YOUR LIFE — HOW TO MAKE THE MOST OF IT

VIDEO CASSETTE PROGRAMS
TIME UNDER CONTROL
MANAGING STRESS

SPEECH REPRINT
"Parenting and Teaching: It's Show Business"

ORDER DIRECTLY FROM THE PUBLISHER

MANDEL PUBLICATIONS
a division of the
Management Development Institute, Inc.
P.O. Box 16432
San Antonio, Texas 78216-1132